Common Sense

A

SHORT

GUIDE

TO

ESSAY

WRITING

Common Sense

A SHORT GUIDE TO ESSAY WRITING

BERNIE GAIDOSCH

George Brown College

Harcourt Brace & Company, Canada

Toronto Montreal Orlando Fort Worth San Diego Philadelphia
London Sydney Tokyo

Canadian Cataloguing in Publication Data
Gaidosch, Bernie
　　　Common sense : a short guide to essay writing

ISBN 0-03-922903-3

1. English language – Rhetoric. 2. Essay.
I. Title.

LB2369.G34 1993　　　808'.042　　　C93-093778-3

Publisher: Heather McWhinney
Editor and Marketing Manager: Michael Young
Developmental Editor: Nancy S. Ennis
Editorial and Marketing Co-ordinator: Kelly Picavet
Director of Publishing Services: Jean Lancee
Editorial Manager: Marcel Chiera
Production Editor: Kathleen M. Vanderlinden
Production Manager: Sue-Ann Becker
Manufacturing Co-ordinator: Denise Wake
Copy Editor: James Leahy
Cover Design: Dave Peters
Cover Photo: Susan Dobson
Interior Design: Dave Peters
Illustrations: William Kimber
Typesetting and Assembly: Debbie Fleming
Printing and Binding: Best Gagné Book Manufacturers

∞ This book was printed in Canada on acid-free paper.
1 2 3 4 5 　　 98 97 96 95 94

This book is dedicated to
my wonderful brother
Wilf Gaidosch
who died of AIDS.
1961–1993

PREFACE

The reality of essay writing is familiar to both teachers and students: namely, that students want to write good essays, but, for some reason, often don't or can't. Some students may have only a limited understanding of essay writing and, consequently, may feel unsure or confused about what the task entails; others may have a clearer sense of what they do when they write an essay but see that process as "artificial" and removed from the way they usually think in everyday situations. As a result, in both cases, writing a good essay remains a mostly inaccessible goal for many students.

Making essay writing accessible is the motivating idea behind *Common Sense: A Short Guide to Essay Writing*. It does so in several ways:

1. It deals with commonly held ideas about essay writing and takes the "mystery" out of the process.

2. It shows the development of an essay in terms of an easy-to-understand answer to a question.

3. It presents a common sense understanding of essay writing as a process grounded in the experience of everyday thinking.

4. It addresses students' emotions around essay writing and tries to take the fear out of the task.

In keeping with the idea of accessibility, the book's approach is direct and open. It is written in straightforward language with a minimum of "technical" terminology. It is also set up as a "reader-friendly" text: the informal headings, the drawings, and the focus sections such as "Spot Checks," "Key Points," and "Highlights" make it easy and enjoyable to use. Similarly, the "Things to Do" activities that follow each section help students to think about, discuss, and use their understanding of what each section is about. Finally, the book's use of humour sets a relaxed tone; the recognizable examples of characters and situations from the worlds of music and television are grounded in broad, common experience and have a wide range of appeal.

You may want to use the chapters and sections out of sequence. For example, the students might read and discuss the section on motivation, "Why You Write," before they tackle the first two chapters on essay writing. That's fine. Feel free to address issues as the need arises.

Many students feel unsure of themselves (and therefore excluded) when they come to write an essay. This book addresses that sense of exclusion by relating to students on a level they can understand and feel a part of. This book helps them see that what they do when they write an essay is similar to what they do when they formulate their opinions in everyday life. Through the use of such techniques as dialogues between two students and examples from music and television, the book develops a common sense approach that aims for a sense of *inclusion* on the part of students.

HELLO AND
WELCOME TO THIS BOOK

During my years as a teacher, I've met many students who were confused about writing an essay. Their confusion would come out in various ways. For instance, they'd say: "What do you want in this essay?" or "How can I write this essay to get the best mark possible?" or "Why did I get only a 'C' again?" These students were neither stupid nor incapable of writing an essay. On the contrary, they were bright and genuinely wanted to "get it right"—to be able to write a good essay. Yet they were confused.

They were confused chiefly because they saw writing an essay as both an abstract and complex task, one they felt either uncomfortable about or incapable of dealing with. What they couldn't see (only because they'd never thought of it in these terms) was that when they wrote an essay *they were actually doing something they had done many times before and were quite familiar with*. But, because they'd never pictured this undertaking in an ordinary, common sense way, they continued to see their task as difficult, if not impossible.

This book is for all those students. If you have ever been confused about essay writing, then this book is for you as well.

In order to make this book as understandable to as many people as possible, I've kept my references to technical writing terms to a minimum and have used as examples situations and essays that readers can readily recognize and enjoy. I've also written the book in a style that is familiar and easy to grasp. My hope is that going through this book is a "fun experience" for you. I've always felt that learning *can* and *should* be fun and that the things we remember the best are those that are the most fun to learn.

ACKNOWLEDGEMENTS

The ideas in this book were worked out over a few years. Along the way, I was fortunate to get helpful suggestions from both student and teacher readers. For these, I'd like to thank the students who shared their views with me: Caroline, Cathy, Brett, Isaac, Jane, Leah, Simon, and Stephanie. I am also grateful for the constructive comments of the reviewers selected by Harcourt Brace & Company: Anita Agar, Kent Baker, Susan Braley, Ricki Heller, Lynn Holmes, Dorothy Kelleher,

Joan Pilz, and Jim Streeter. As well, my thanks go to these people: to my editors, Heather McWhinney, Michael Young, Nancy S. Ennis, Kathleen M. Vanderlinden, and my copy editor, James Leahy; to my friends, John Clelland for his early support of the book, Larry Hopperton for his ongoing advice, and Diana Schouten for her word processing skills; and to my wife, Maureen, for her proofreading and loving support. Finally, I thank my mother, Irma, my best teacher ever.

A NOTE FROM THE PUBLISHER

Thank you for selecting *Common Sense: A Short Guide to Essay Writing* by Bernie Gaidosch. The author and publisher have devoted considerable time to the careful development of this book. We appreciate your recognition of this effort and accomplishment.

We want to hear what you think about *Common Sense: A Short Guide to Essay Writing*. Please take a few minutes to fill in the stamped reply card at the back of the book. Your comments and suggestions will be valuable to us as we prepare new editions and other books.

CONTENTS

5 MAKING YOUR ESSAY WORK   115

CHAPTER 1

LOOKING AT AN ESSAY

SOME PLAIN TALK ABOUT ESSAYS

Picture these three scenes:

You're learning how to ride a two-wheel bicycle. The training wheels are off and your mom or dad is jogging along with you, holding on to the back of the bike's seat to make sure you stay balanced. Your heart feels heavy in your chest, but at the same time it's thumping ten times faster than your feet going around on the pedals. The wind is in your hair and in your eyes and you're not really sure how you're doing. You're wondering if you can do this at all, wondering if you'll fall and hurt yourself, wondering if you'll *ever* learn how to ride ... and the wind in your face is suddenly pushing out tears from the corners of your eyes.

You're going out on your first date. You've taken lots of time to get ready for THE BIG EVENT. You've primped and posed and preened in the mirror to some level of satisfaction from every conceivable angle. Despite the "picture of perfection" that's reflected back to you, doubts remain: "How do I *really* look?" "Is my hair all right?" "What if I'm too nervous?" "Are my palms sweating?" "What if ...?" Then the doorbell sounds and your pulse rate goes into "Fast Forward."

You're sitting in class, gazing lazily out the window at nothing in particular when the teacher gives out the big term assignment — THE MAJOR RESEARCH ESSAY. A cold, icy feeling starts in your feet then rises quickly to your heart, throat, and brain. You suddenly realize that you have to write an essay, and the vague terror of that thought leaves you numb and breathless.

What emotion is common to all three of these events? Is it nervousness, anticipation, excitement? Certainly it's all of these.

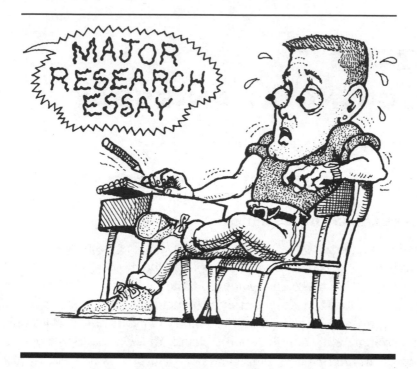

But the butterflies in the stomach, the sweaty palms, the racing heart, all come from something deeper: *fear*. Fear is a natural reaction that can come from many things. These things don't even have to be unusual or dangerous. As these examples show, fear can easily come from doing everyday, ordinary things. Fear can come from learning to ride a bicycle, going out on a first date, or having to write an essay. And, while you eventually learn to cope with the first two events, having to write an essay is something that can create fear in you over many years.

The cause of your fear in all these situations is uncertainty. You're uncertain when you're learning to ride a bicycle because you don't know if you'll fall off and hurt yourself; you're uncertain on your first date because you don't know what's expected of you and are afraid of rejection; and you are uncertain when you write an essay because you're unsure of what you're doing and are afraid of failing. Life's experiences usually teach you how to deal with bicycles and romance — but life's experiences are rarely enough to teach you how to cope with writing an essay and to feel good about the process.

But while fear may be a natural response to writing an essay, it's certainly not a necessary response — as long as you understand what an essay is in its simplest, most basic terms. What you will find is that writing an essay can become as natural as balancing a bike or saying "goodnight" to your date.

It may strike you as odd, though, to suggest that fear might be a natural consequence of writing an essay. If fear comes from writing an essay, you might think, can it really be a fear of something you're uncertain about? You may readily see that fear could arise from learning the intricacies of bike balancing or from learning how to survive your first major social encounter, but isn't an essay something that you already know about?

Don't you know, for instance, that you have to read about the topic, that you have to figure out what you're going to say, and that you have to "fill" a certain number of pages with words? Haven't you been asked to write essays for most of the time you've been at school? If so, then haven't you become familiar (even grudgingly) with what an essay is, with what's expected of you when you have to write one?

Well, the answer is *yes* — and *no*. *Yes*, because for many years you've heard about essays from other people who seem to know what an essay is, who assign essays with all sorts of expectations attached to them, and who feel comfortable when talking about essays. This continual exposure gives you the sense that you, too, know what an essay is and that you, too, *ought* to feel comfortable when writing one.

But do you? Well, this is where the *no* comes in. If, after all this exposure to essays, you still don't feel sure about what you're doing when you're writing one, the reason is probably quite simple: you don't see what an essay is in exactly the same way as the person who assigns one sees it.

This doesn't mean that you're thick-headed. What it means is that you don't have the same *perception* of what an essay is. Look at it this way.

Teachers who have worked with essays for many years have developed a clear sense of an essay. They then try their best to pass on that understanding to you, who haven't grappled with the task for nearly as long a time. While *some* of the teacher's explanation is conveyed and understood, often a great deal of misunderstanding on your part remains.

The teacher's purpose is to get you to look at an essay as a precise, structured, and unified expression of your thoughts on a subject, but unfortunately this way of thinking and expressing your thoughts may seem all too alien to the way in which you usually look at and think about things. Approaching an essay in this way can leave you with a feeling similar to that of walking into a museum, an art gallery, or a cathedral for the first time. You probably have a vague sense that you like what you see, but at the same time you're so overwhelmed by the immensity or complexity of it all that you end up speaking in whispered and reverential tones about it and casting nervous and doubtful glances all around.

So, then, what perception of an essay should you have? How do you make sense of your teachers' precise, structured, and unified view of an essay? How can you get from where you are to where they are?

Well, that's what this book is about. It shows that no one is far from understanding what an essay is in the first place. It's a common sense guide that sees essay writing as a natural extension of the way in which you think every day of your life and of how you come to form your opinions about things. It suggests that there really is no difference between your teachers' view of an essay and your own ability to come up with opinions and ideas. One may be called "formal" thinking and the other "informal" thinking, but essentially they are the same process and can lead to the same result. If you can see the connection between what you do when you write an essay and your everyday thinking processes, then you'll be able to eliminate any fear around the task and feel confident and comfortable when you have to write an essay.

The alternative is not a happy one. The alternative is that you continue what you have been doing — that you guess when you're writing an essay, that you "fake it." This doesn't mean that you don't know what you're doing but that you are unclear about something you needn't be unclear about at all.

For many people, learning to write an essay is very much a hit-and-miss experience. You write something, get it back with a mark and comments, read the comments, incorporate the teacher's suggestions in your next essay, get the essay back, and so on.

Essentially, there's nothing wrong with this process. In fact, it's the way most learning happens. The only problem with it, though, is that it takes a long time (often many years) before you reach a level of clarity (with a corresponding level of confidence) about understanding essays.

That's the reason for this book. It's a "shortcut," but not in the cheap sense of the word. It's a shortcut in the sense that it shows in clear terms and straightforward language what an essay is. Its goal is to clarify for you what essay writing is and to guide you in doing it. Read on and see.

WHAT AN ESSAY IS NOT

Before we talk about what an essay is, we should mention briefly *what an essay is not*. Although your teachers have a clear sense of an essay, all too often you come away with only a vague idea of what's expected of you, of what you're being asked to do. In short, you can develop ideas about what an essay is not.

To hear these ideas is quite revealing. Most of the time, they sound reasonable enough, but on a regular basis they don't yield the kinds of results you would be happy with. What are these ideas? They come in different forms, but two of the most common ones are what I call "the mechanical view" and "the empty vessel view."

THE MECHANICAL VIEW

This view of an essay deals with the basic components of an essay: the parts that are commonly called the introduction, the body, and the conclusion. You usually have some understanding of these parts of an essay, but, when you write an essay, you deal with them *separately* from each other because you've learned that these are the constituent parts of an essay — that when they're put together they make up the whole essay.

The trouble with this approach is that often these parts don't hold together when the essay is finished. For example, suppose your essay topic asks whether or not irrigation methods used by farmers in Ethiopia are adequate. Your introduction might say that the methods are adequate, the body of the essay might give examples to show that some methods are adequate and that some are inadequate, and, finally, the conclusion might state that the methods are definitely *inadequate*.

The logical thing to do in this case would be to rewrite the essay, since the three parts don't say the same thing to the reader, and the reader is ultimately left confused. However, even the most capable and well-intentioned student may think, "Well, it says *sort of* what I wanted it to say," and then hand in the essay. When this happens, the teacher might comment that the essay has "great potential — if only more work had been done with it, it could have been much better" or that "you finally get around to saying something at the end, but what about the first third or half of the essay?"

The trouble here, then, comes from having a "mechanical" view of an essay. The introduction, body, and conclusion become similar to, say, the mechanical parts of an old clock that somehow fit together but can't be made to work in an integrated way. In other words, you write the three parts of the essay and then can't get them to say the same thing. The question behind this view of an essay — and one that is frequently voiced — is "How do I make the parts fit together?" The difficulty you might have in "fitting them together" is usually the result of seeing these parts as distinct and separate components of a whole essay.

THE EMPTY VESSEL VIEW

In this view of an essay, you usually don't even think about the introduction, body, and conclusion. Instead, you might rush to the library, read whatever books you can find on the topic, and then, through some "magical" process, take in all you've read and pour it back onto the empty pages of your essay. The important thing becomes the quantity of words, not the quality of thinking.

In this case, you may view the essay as some kind of empty vessel or container, and your only concern is finding a way to "fill" it with enough words that have something to do with the topic. The usual question behind this view of an essay is "How do I fill five or ten empty pages?"

The result of this approach is again one of confusion on the part of the reader. The feedback here may come in the form of these comments: "You've got some interesting material here, but you don't do anything with it" or "I can see that you've done your research, but you need to give the essay some focus." The problem comes from loading the pages with words and not giving much thought as to whether the words actually *say* something, actually put forth a logical point of view. You may think, "As long as there are words on these pages, the essay is finished. I've done my job."

If you see yourself in these descriptions, that's all right. You're not alone. If you see an essay in either "mechanical" or "empty vessel" terms, your feelings about it are usually the result of uncertainty about what you're doing. You may even write the essay out of a feeling of wanting to get it over with. You may have a sense of what you're trying to do but, out of desperation, you see your choices as (1) haphazardly patching the essay together or (2) putting it off to the last minute and then rushing to get it done. Your attitude toward the essay is less a desire to understand the topic better than a sense of relief at handing it in, at handing *anything* in. Then, when you get the essay back with a "C" or a "D," you're not pleased with the result, but are at least relieved that you passed and that you don't have to do *that* assignment again.

Unfortunately, this process is usually repeated the next time you have to write an essay, so the feelings of frustration and desperation only become deeper over time. As a result, whenever a teacher even mentions the word "essay," you may experience the feelings mentioned at the beginning of this book — uncertainty and fear. But this need not be the case. Indeed, in the next section, you'll see that having a "mechanical" or "empty vessel" view of an essay is not the only option — a better one does exist.

WHAT AN ESSAY IS

There is a better way to understand what an essay is. And the basis for this understanding begins with a close look at *the relationship between an essay and an essay topic.*

When you're given an essay topic, how do you usually react? If you react with fear and uncertainty, then your response to the topic will be based on these emotions. In other words, you'll probably react in a way similar to the "mechanical" or "empty vessel" views. You'll try to "load up" your pages with information without giving too much thought to how you're doing it.

In order to approach an essay topic in a more thoughtful way, it's necessary to take a good look at the essay topic itself, and ask yourself, "What is this topic asking me to do?" Well, if you view an essay topic *in its simplest terms*, you quickly see that any topic — no matter how long it is — usually asks a question: "Are the irrigation methods used by farmers in Ethiopia adequate?"

What the essay itself is, then, in relation to the essay topic, is an answer to some particular question. The relationship can be seen in this way:

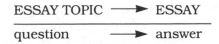

ESSAY TOPIC ⟶ ESSAY

question ⟶ answer

In its simplest terms, *an essay is no more than an answer to a question.* What you're doing when you're writing an essay is responding to someone's question about some topic. The topic may be presented directly in question form or it may be presented as a dilemma, a problem that requires a solution. In that case, the relationship would look like this:

ESSAY TOPIC ⟶ ESSAY

problem ⟶ solution

In this form, the problem would be worded differently — "Discuss the irrigation methods of farmers in Ethiopia" — but it would still ask you for a response (an answer) to the essay topic. Understanding the relationship between an essay topic and an essay in these basic terms is understanding what an essay is.

But, while understanding this relationship is not a complex understanding, it's a very important one. It's important because it lets you see that, when teachers assign an essay topic, all they really want you to do is to respond to it — to answer some question.

"Well," you might stop to think here, "this may be so, but isn't this already obvious?" or "Haven't I heard about this as a thesis statement before?" or "How can knowing this help me write an essay?"

Let's look at an everyday example to consider *the process involved in giving an answer*. Let's listen in on a conversation between two students, Tina and Tom, having a beer in the pub after classes are over.

Tina:	So, you're really into rock music, eh?
Tom:	Yeah, I guess I am.
Tina:	So, like, in your opinion, which is the most popular rock group?
Tom:	That's easy — The Rolling Stones!
Tina:	The Rolling Stones! You mean The Strolling Bones! Those guys are so ancient they're almost dead! Where'd you hear about them — in History class?
Tom:	Oh, go ahead and laugh. But, really, I think they are far and away the most popular band ever. In fact, I think they're the one and only rock band that can claim that distinction. I think that ....
Tina:	Whoa! Hold it. Slow down. What you say really interests me. I'll tell you what. Let me buy you another beer, and you can tell me what makes you think these guys are so popular.

 SPOT CHECK

Let's stop here and do an analysis or "spot check." Ask yourself if, in this informal situation, you have a question and an answer. You probably don't have to think too long to see that the question in this conversation is something like this: "Which is the most popular rock group?" and that the answer is "I think that the most popular rock group is The Rolling Stones."

Can you also say, then, that the question in this example is the same thing as an essay topic and that the answer is the same thing as an essay? Well, at first glance, perhaps not.

After all, an essay topic asks you for your view about a particular subject, doesn't it? But, if this is true, then doesn't the question "Which is the most popular rock group?" ask for an opinion, a view of a particular subject? Of course it does. Thus, it does the same thing an essay topic does.

In the same way, isn't the response "I think that the most popular rock group is The Rolling Stones" an answer to the question "Which is the most popular rock group?" Of course it is.

But if, as you're seeing, an essay is an answer to a question, does that make the answer "I think that the most popular rock group is The Rolling Stones" an essay? At first glance, the answer to this is clearly *no* — an essay does more than provide only a one-sentence answer. So, then, if this response isn't an essay as you know it, what does it need to become one? Let's go back to the conversation and follow it further to see how it develops.

Tom:	Wow, that's great! Sure I'll have another beer. So, what makes the group so popular? Well, a lot of things.
Tina:	What do you mean, "a lot of things?" Name some. I mean, be specific.
Tom:	Well, let's see. For one, there's the group's profile — I mean, they're *so* recognizable. Take Mick Jagger's vocals — when he's singing, you just *know* who's singing. You don't have to be told. And also Keith Richards's intro guitar licks on a song like "Jumpin' Jack Flash." As soon as you hear that guitar — DUDU DUDU DUDUDUDU — you *know* that music. But another reason they're so popular is the band's longevity — you said it yourself when you called them "ancient." They've been a force in rock music on a steady basis for around 30 years. Thirty years! Think of how many groups have come and gone while these guys just roll on. Then, there's the band's record sales and earnings throughout the

	world. We're talking big numbers here — for sure over 100 million records sold in over 50 countries. That's a lot of records and a lot of people! The volume is so great that by sheer numbers alone these guys are an industry by themselves!
Tina:	Well, you certainly do have some ideas on this subject.
Tom:	Yeah, I guess I've heard a lot of it from my mom.

Are you any closer to recognizing Tom's answer as an essay now? Certainly, he's given a more detailed answer to the question than he did in his first reply. This time, he's given not only his *view* on the subject, but he's also given his *reasons* behind the view. In short, he's told Tina *what* he thinks and *why* he thinks it.

So, then, what he's started to do is develop the ideas on which his answer is based. And that, as you know, is pretty much what you do when you write an essay. *When you write an essay, what you actually do is give an answer to a question (an essay that responds to an essay topic) with reasons to back it up.* So you're starting to see some similarity here between Tom's answer (with its reasons) and an essay.

But is that enough? For instance, are Tom's reasons as fully developed as they could be? Do they appear in any specific order of importance? The answer to these questions is clearly *no*. But you do have a start. You have a framework to make this an essay. Let's listen again to see what happens when Tom develops one of his points.

Tina:	I guess parents are good for some things. But which of these reasons would you really stick with — which is the one that's the most important?
Tom:	That's a tough one. It's hard to choose. But, if I had to narrow it down, I'd say it's the group's record sales and earnings over the years. I mean the other things are important too — recognizability and longevity have lots to do with popularity — but it's the numbers here that are the most important reason for why The Stones are the most popular group. Look at it this way. In the 30 or so years that they've been around, The Stones have sold over 100 million records in more than 50 countries around the world.

In addition, they've had more than 50 Number 1 hits on the charts, and their recent "Steel Wheels Tour" grossed over $100 million in less than six months! No other rock band has ever come close to these figures in any of these categories. Really, Tina, the numbers speak for themselves. The popularity of this band on the basis of hard numbers is incredible and in a class by itself!

Is this response any different from what Tom has given before? In one sense it isn't different because he still maintains — on the basis of the group's record sales and earnings — that The Rolling Stones are the most popular rock group. In other words, his answer to the question is still the same. In another way, though, this response *is* different from his previous ones in the sense that he develops one of his reasons much more fully than he did before.

It's in this development of Tom's reason, then, that you can start to see a resemblance between his casual responses and the structure of an essay. And that resemblance looks something like this:

1. Tom's opinion in its simplest form (that The Rolling Stones are the most popular rock group) is *the essence of the essay itself*; it's his answer to Tina's question, "Which is the most popular rock group?" and it's what he tries to prove to her with his reasons.

2. The reasons Tom gives Tina are the basis for why he thinks what he does and, in simple form, are what he tells her to convince her of his point of view; a simple list of these reasons actually resembles the main points you choose in an essay to persuade your readers.

3. Tom's elaboration of the point about the group's "record sales and earnings" is a further attempt to show Tina more of his chief reason for thinking the way he does about this topic; his development of this reason is the same thing you do when you develop your reasons in an essay.

If you look at the "bare bones" of Tina's question and Tom's answer in terms of an *outline*, it would look something like this:

Which is the most popular rock group?	QUESTION
The most popular rock group is The Rolling Stones.	ANSWER
The Rolling Stones are the most popular rock group because of:	REASONS

- their recognizability
- their longevity
- their record sales and earnings

The most important thing that makes The Rolling Stones the most popular group is their record sales and earnings:

- over 100 million records sold in over 50 countries worldwide

- 50 Number 1 hits

- "Steel Wheels Tour" grossed over $100 million in less than 6 months

What you're seeing here is that Tom's answer (or essay) to Tina's question (or essay topic) is unchanged throughout. Had he been asked what his answer was at any point in the conversation he could only have replied: "The most popular rock band is The Rolling Stones." You're also seeing, though, that Tom has reasons (his points) to back up what he thinks and that, when challenged, he can say something in depth about any one of those reasons.

In both of these ways, then, Tom's answer to the question bears a strong resemblance to what you do when you write an essay. Does that mean that his answer (as far as he's given it) *is* an essay? Well, he's certainly off to a good start. He has an answer (what he's trying to prove), he has some points to support his answer, and he's thought carefully about at least one of those points. But is that enough? Let's listen again.

Tina:	Well, that's quite impressive! I didn't think you'd given this much thought to the topic.
Tom:	I guess I'm just interested in rock music and have some strong views about it.
Tina:	You're right — you do have some strong views. But it's not just that. As I said, your ideas are quite well thought out too. Humm.... I'll tell you what. I've just had an idea that may be able to help you and someone else at the same time. How would you like to make $300?
Tom:	$300! Wow! What do I have to do?
Tina:	Just what you've been doing. I have a friend who works for the newspaper, and she's doing a series on something like "the fan's view of music." She's been getting music fans of all types to submit essays to the paper on their views. The paper pays $300 for each essay that's chosen to be printed. From what

> you've told me, I see no reason why you can't write an essay on your view of The Rolling Stones and send it to the newspaper.
>
> *Tom:*   Wow! I'll rush home and start on it right now!
>
> *Tina:*   Just a minute — it looks like I forgot my wallet. Can you pay for these beers?

All right, where has this conversation finally arrived? Well, through her suggestion, Tina has ultimately provided the way for Tom to turn his answer into an essay. She has put him in the position of wanting *to write out his answer on paper.* This is a major step in the process you've been watching. The reason is that when Tom writes out his answer on paper, he's doing several important things:

1. He is focusing on his answer — he's asking himself clearly, "What am I trying to prove?" Once he knows what it is he's trying to prove, he should put this statement into one sentence and keep it near him while he's writing.

2. He is thinking of reasons to back up his answer in order to convince his readers to see things as he does.

3. Since he probably won't use all of his reasons, he needs to eliminate some and put the remaining ones into the best possible order.

4. He has to develop his reasons sufficiently so that his readers will be convinced when they read them.

When Tom got through the process of putting his ideas down on paper and sent his essay to the newspaper, the result looked like this:

The Rolling Stones — The Most Popular Rock Group Ever

Compared to all the rock bands that have come and gone over the years, The Rolling Stones are the one band that seems to have always been on the music scene. Since the early '60s, when they came out with their first hit single "Not Fade Away," to their recent grand-scale "Steel Wheels Tour," The Rolling Stones have gained worldwide popularity with several generations of fans. And, at the root of this popularity are three factors that show why The Stones are so great:

their music and singing are instantly recognizable, they've been together for a long time, and their volume of record sales and earnings
is the greatest for any rock group ever.

There's no other rock group that has as many instantly recognizable tunes as The Stones. While the quality of Keith Richards's guitar
playing is undeniable, resulting in songs that are all different enough
to be new each time out, there's also an unmistakable "Stones
signature" to each. Guitar "licks" on songs such as "Gimme Shelter,"
"Satisfaction," and "Miss You" all trigger immediate "ah-ha" reactions in many people. The same can be said for the vocal side of the
combination — Mick Jagger's voice. There are few other voices in the
world of rock music that are as much the stamp of a certain group
to as many people as his voice is. Whether we hear Jagger's voice on
the most popular songs such as "Honky Tonk Woman," "Paint It
Black," or "Jumpin' Jack Flash" or on lesser-known songs like "Wild
Horses" or "Midnight Rambler," that hard-edged, gravelly voice is
recognizable to millions.

Another thing that makes this group the most popular is its
longevity — the length of time they've been together. The Stones
started their music careers as part of the "British invasion" of rock
bands in the early '60s and, while the band has been through changes
in personnel (with the death of Brian Jones in 1969 and the on-
again–off-again presence of players like Ron Wood), they've continued
as a strong musical force through the '60s, '70s, '80s, and now
into the '90s. Over the years, some of the people in the band such
as drummer Charlie Watts and singer Mick Jagger have even pursued
solo careers, but, for some reason or other, they always come back to
that "thing" that seems to have a life of its own: The Rolling Stones.
Now, as they enter their fourth decade as a rock band, their "Steel
Wheels Tour" has given "the rock band that stayed together the
longest" a new vitality and a new audience around the world. There
can be no doubt about this point. The long time The Stones have been
together speaks for itself and is concrete proof that they've out-
lasted all the competition.

The most important reason for the popularity of The Rolling
Stones, though, is their record sales and earnings. On a worldwide
basis, these guys have out-sold and out-earned every other rock
band ever. In the 30 or so years that they've been around, The Stones

have sold over 100 million records in more than 50 countries around the world. In addition, they've had more than 50 Number 1 hits on the charts and their "Steel Wheels Tour" grossed over $100 million in less than six months. No other rock band has even come close to any of these figures in any of these categories. These numbers are hard facts and are proof positive of the vast appeal of The Stones.

There can't really be any doubt about this issue — The Rolling Stones are unquestionably the most popular rock group ever. Their recognizability, longevity, and sales are the ingredients that combine to account for the band's success over the past 30 years. And, judging by their latest successes, it looks like their popularity will continue with new generations of fans throughout the world for years to come.

Our spot check of this process leads to some important points:

★ **KEY POINTS**

1. It's clear from this essay that Tom has come a long way from his original, simple answer. It's also clear from this essay that its essence is still only that simple answer: the most popular rock group is The Rolling Stones.

2. By writing out his answer, Tom has come to *formalize* his previously casual thoughts on this topic. By writing the essay for the newspaper, he is turning the thoughts he usually expressed only in conversation into a formal presentation of his view on The Rolling Stones. In this everyday example of the way you most often express yourself, then, you see the actual process through which essay writing takes place — *Tom's development of his idea about the Rolling Stones is exactly the same process you go through when you think out an idea for yourself or for an essay.* And the central aspect of this process — its most important feature — is the fact that an essay is no more than an answer to a question.

3. No matter what its length, any essay grows out of a clear and specific answer to an essay topic. Consequently, you can *expand* your one-sentence answer either by thinking of more points to support your view and/or by developing more fully those points you may have or any new ones you can think of. On the other hand, you should be able to *reduce* any essay to its essence, to the clarity of a single sentence: "This essay is trying to prove that ...." Once you understand the simplicity of expanding a simple answer into an essay or, conversely, contracting an essay into a simple answer, then you can see that what you *do* when you write an essay is no different from how you respond when someone asks you for your view of something. You may give a long or a short response, but you still give only an answer.

If you understand the power that this flexibility gives you, you'll gradually come to see that there's nothing to fear when you are faced with writing an essay. You can replace this fear with the confidence that comes from knowing what an essay is.

☼ HIGHLIGHTS

- An essay is an answer to a question.
- Once you know what you're trying to prove, you have to state it as clearly as possible.
- When you have your answer, you can develop it into an essay of any length.
- You should be able to take an essay of any length and reduce it to a single sentence.

✍ THINGS TO DO

1. See if you can express these things in one-sentence answers. Try to say "what the whole thing was about":

a) an advertisement that you find effective

b) a movie you saw

c) a current issue in the newspaper

d) a song you like on the radio

e) a music video that interests you

f) a TV program

Now write down two or three main points behind each response.

Discuss your findings in class. Compare your responses with those of other students.

2. Search out an article in either a newspaper or a magazine. State what it's about in one sentence. Pick out two or three reasons to back up what you think the article is saying.

Can you make up an essay topic that this article would be a response to? Try this in class with another person. Each of you can respond to the same article and then compare your answers and your essay topics to see what you came up with.

3. Look at an essay topic that you're working on now. Does it ask a question? Or does it give a dilemma or situation as a problem to be solved? Try to come up with a one-sentence answer to reply to it. When you have an answer, then think of two or three reasons to back it up. Try this with a friend's essay.

Do this in class with your essay and a friend's.

4. Read these two student essays. Write down what each one is about in a one-sentence answer. To check if your answer is a good one, write down two or three points that you would use to back it up.

Video Games Are a Hit

When video games first came out on the market about 20 years ago, the public didn't pay too much attention to them. Since the early '80s, however, they've become the hit of that (and this) decade.

When we look at why they've been so popular and successful, three reasons are apparent: they're entertaining, educational, and profitable. For these reasons, video games became popular with the public in a very short time.

Kids were the first ones to "go wild" over video games. These games were new and entertaining and were not expensive to play. Parents also liked video games because their children were being entertained; the games kept children occupied and out of trouble while exposing them to computers. Home video game systems such as Atari and Nintendo were quickly introduced, and parents started buying them so that kids could stay home and play their favourites. The games became a "cheap" form of entertainment and the whole family ended up playing them together, be it computer ping-pong, chess, or even some version of Space Invaders.

By the '80s, we had entered the computer age, but even in the midst of all the confusion about computers, no one could deny the educational aspect of these games. When playing a game, even if it was a "kill 'em all" kind of game like Asteroids or Pac-Man, players were being exposed to computer use and were becoming ever more "friendly" with computers. The days of the public being shy or afraid of computers, or of seeing them as a threat to society, were over. Instead, by playing with them, people gradually began to see computers as the educational tool they have become today.

But families were not the only ones caught up in the video game "mania." Video games were big profit makers, and business people started investing heavily in the industry. Computer programmers such as Jim Butterfield started dedicating all their time to creating newer and better games in order to capitalize on this craze. Even traditionally respectable educational computer companies such as Commodore and Apple began concentrating heavily in this field, and suddenly the "video game war" was on.

Video games have clearly become big winners. They have the winning combination of being entertaining, educational, and profitable. They are bound to be around for a long time, become even better and more appealing, and affect the lives of a great many people in one way or another.

Women Are Superior to Men

There is little question that an average adult male is physically superior to a woman in strength, speed, and muscle mass. But, in some areas, women have a distinct advantage over men. The areas for which this is the case are as follows: female babies are more likely to survive birth trauma and infant diseases than are male babies; studies have shown that women, as a group, react better in stressful situations and overcome emotional crises better than men do; and women on average outlive men by approximately five years.

Research has proved that the newborn male child is more susceptible to infection and disease than newborn females are. Scientists have discovered that, initially, a male child's immune system (and thus his resistance) is not as strong as a female's. This imbalance soon evens out after the first month or so, but at the beginning of life, it is the female who has the stronger constitution.

Furthermore, through the middle years, women are better able to cope with stress and stressful situations than men are. According to researchers, men have a higher rate of stroke and heart disease than do women, and in both areas stress is at least partially responsible. Also, more men die of lung disease because of smoking, one cause of which is once again stress. Even in the case of the death of a mate, it has been shown that women cope better than men and live longer after the death of a mate.

Finally, near the end of life, women again assert their superiority. Life insurance statistics show that, in general, women outlive men by approximately five years (and that span is increasing steadily). Today, for example, a woman's life span is about 80 years while a man's is only about 75. Men tend to have a higher incidence of stroke, heart disease, and cancer — all of which account for their shorter life expectancy.

To say that women are "the weaker sex," then, is not entirely accurate. They may be weaker in some areas, but in many other important ones, they are clearly superior to men.

CHAPTER 2

UNDERSTANDING HOW AN ESSAY WORKS

KNOWING WHAT AN ESSAY IS CAN HELP YOU WHEN YOU HAVE TO WRITE ONE

Knowing that an essay is just an answer to a question can clarify the often mystifying process of writing an essay and turn it into a manageable task. The next step, then, is to apply this knowledge to the way an essay develops and the best approach to take when you have to write one.

To better understand how to tackle the job of writing an essay, let's start with a look at the three main parts of an essay. These three parts are, of course, the introduction, the body, and the conclusion. Take a look at these parts as they're listed here and number them in the order in which you would write them when you're working on an essay:

Introduction

Body

Conclusion

When asked to do this, most students number the parts in the following way, although other variations are possible:

1. Introduction

2. Body

3. Conclusion

This response isn't unusual; in fact, it's the one given most often be-cause *it's the one learned most often.* You go through school learning that you write your introduction to an essay first, the body second, and the conclusion third. You learn to start at "the beginning" and end at "the end." Because this sounds reasonable enough, you think that there's nothing wrong with writing the parts of an essay in this order. You think this way, that is, until you see the results.

What generally happens is that you begin well enough, but, about a third or half of the way through the essay, you change your mind about your answer (what you're trying to prove) and write about another view-point for the remainder of the essay. You begin with one reasonable-sounding idea, write about it for a while, then find it leads to another idea (one that's usually closer to what you believe is the answer) and then write about the new idea for the rest of the essay.

This change in direction often results in a grade of "C" or "D," and the teacher's response might be something like this: "For the first part of the essay, it looks as though you're only warming up to what you want to say; but it's not till you're halfway through that you finally get around to actually saying it. From that point on, this is a fine essay. Just rethink what you're doing here." Well, let's do that now. Let's rethink what you're doing here.

Think about changing the order of the three parts of an essay so that the essay is an answer to a question. Consider this order:

1. Conclusion
2. Body
3. Introduction

At first, it may seem odd to write the parts of an essay in the *reverse* order. It may indeed seem odd until you recall our starting point: that an essay is an answer to a question.

THE CONCLUSION

Why should you start working on the conclusion first? Isn't this going at it backwards? Well, when you know that an essay is an answer, then you can think about the conclusion as *the answer itself* — the conclusion of your essay is the thing that you're trying to prove, the point to which you're trying to bring your reader. At the same time, because it's the point that *you* arrive at first (because you've already figured out the answer), it should be your natural starting point when you write your essay.

Let's think about this view. In the conversation between Tina and Tom, the point that Tom was trying to make was that "The Rolling Stones are the most popular rock band." Similarly, in his essay, the point to which Tom tried to bring his readers can be found in his conclusion: that The Stones are the most popular rock band. In other words, Tom had to know what he wanted to prove (had to know his answer to Tina's question) *before* he could start to prove it to her. He had to work through what he'd learned about The Stones, draw his conclusion from that information, then present his conclusion as the answer to Tina's question.

If he doesn't know what his conclusion is, he might end up spending some time (let's say half of his answer or his essay) dealing with rock groups in general, then debating the merits of rock music versus pop, then going through a history of rock music, and *finally* presenting (in the second half of the essay) his response that The Stones are the most popular rock group. It's just this kind of waffling, or moving from one idea to another, that can happen when you write an essay.

But, if you know your answer, then you have your conclusion. You know exactly what you're trying to prove to your reader, where you're trying to take your reader. But how do you get there? How do you know what your conclusion is when you may be unfamiliar with the particular topic you've been assigned? For the answers to these questions, let's do another spot check of the conversation between Tina and Tom.

✿ SPOT CHECK

How did Tom arrive at his answer, "The Rolling Stones are the most popular rock band"? Where did he get the information that helped him form his answer? What did he do with that information once he got it? Did he benefit from any direct experience?

Consider the possibilities. First, it makes sense to say that Tom could have formed some of his views from having heard The Rolling Stones' music. Second, he could also have learned about the band by reading about them or by seeing them on television or in a film. Third, he might well have formed his idea from talking about them with family or friends. Fourth, he might have even gone to see them at a concert. What do all these things add up to then?

Well, Tom's interest in rock music in general and in The Rolling Stones in particular probably developed gradually on several levels over a period of time and for no specific reason. In other words, he probably never said to himself, "Gee, I'd better find out everything I can about The Rolling Stones in case someday, somewhere, some-one asks me what I think about them." (Such behaviour would be somewhat compulsive, to say the least.) No, what he did was simply follow a natural interest in something and use the information he learned to form an idea about it. This learning about his topic was the process he went through *to reach his conclusion,* and he could arrive at it only after having learned something about his topic.

But how did he learn what he did? Looking back, he may have *read* about the band, *heard* their music, *seen* them in a film or at a con-cert, *talked* about them, and *thought* about them. Read, hear, see, talk, think. These are the things that Tom did.

But how did he do them? On what level did he do them? Well, certainly *not* on a *formal* level. That is, no one assigned him a topic to explore having to do with The Rolling Stones. What he actually did was explore this area of interest casually, on an *informal* level. This is, in fact, what you do with most things in life. You come across information on topics that interest you and, over time, keep adding to the informal "files" you have in your mind. You come to form opinions or views on these topics and, from time to time, may change your views depending on what new information you've learned. Also, at any point in this ongoing process, you're usually quite capable of giving (and quite eager to give) your view of the topic when you're asked.

This is what happened when Tina asked Tom about The Rolling Stones. He gave her his view about the topic she'd raised and which he'd come to a conclusion about.

This gathering, filtering, and sifting of information is exactly the same thing that you do on a formal level when you do research for an essay. You go through information on a topic you may be unfamiliar with and sort it out for yourself, keeping and discarding information, and finally forming your answer about the topic. You can say, then, that whether it is carried out for informal or formal reasons, the learning and thinking that you do on any topic leads you to your conclusion — your answer — and you have to know this conclusion first before you can go back to prove it either in a conversation or an essay.

★ KEY POINTS

1. The informal "research" that you do on a daily basis for the things that interest you is really the same process that you carry out when you're asked to do formal research for an essay. The only real difference between them is that one is done casually and the other is carried out for a specific purpose. You still do the same things to get your information (read, hear, see,

and talk) and you still *do the same thing with the information:* think. Formalizing your research for an essay just takes all these everyday activities one step further — in an essay, you eventually have *to write* about your topic.

2. Whether the research you do is informal or formal, *you have to go through some research process first before you can arrive at your conclusion.* You can't just pluck an answer out of the air or convincingly support someone else's answer ("My mom says The Stones are the most popular rock group, so I'd better think so too") because there's simply nothing behind these "views" except the answer itself. Logically, your research is your only way of getting to your conclusion. Only when you've figured out something for yourself can you explain it to someone else.

3. Once you've reached your conclusion through your research, *you have the starting point for your essay.* You then know what you want to prove to your reader and how you came to believe in that point of view. It's only when you know these two things — what your conclusion is and how you arrived at it — that you can with any certainty turn to your reader and make a case for why they should agree with you. Thus, the conclusion becomes the starting point when it comes time to actually write the essay.

4. Once you know what your conclusion is, you have to be sure to *state it strongly,* in no uncertain terms. Since this is your answer, the point to which you're bringing your reader, it should be the strongest expression of your certainty about what you're trying to prove. Look back to Tom's essay to see how firmly he states his view in the last paragraph (page 14). After announcing his answer in the introduction and supporting it in the body, Tom drives his point home as emphatically as he can in the conclusion.

5. When you have your conclusion, there is a simple but necessary thing you should always do to prevent yourself from straying away from it: *you should write it out in one sentence and keep that piece of paper near when you're writing the essay (in*

the same way as you did with your thesis statement). While you eventually develop your conclusion fully in a paragraph, this sentence is your direction to yourself. By looking at it often, you're continually reminding yourself of where you're going with your topic, and your chances of wandering off topic will be greatly reduced. Also, if you change your mind about the topic while you're writing the essay, you can easily change your answer. Just throw out the piece of paper with your conclusion on it and write down your new conclusion in one sentence. At all times, keep your focus clear and near.

☼ HIGHLIGHTS

- The conclusion to any essay is really the essence of the answer: it's "what I'm trying to prove to my reader" or "where I'm trying to lead my reader."

- You arrive at your conclusion only after you do some basic things first — read, hear, see, talk; you read about, hear about, see, or talk about your topic or area of interest; after doing these things, you think about your topic and form a view about it.

- When you're asked to write an essay about something, you go through the same research and thinking process that you go through every day with things you're familiar with and naturally interested in.

- Your conclusion is the starting point of your essay; when you reach your conclusion you "backtrack" to deal with the body and the introduction.

- Write out your conclusion in one sentence and keep it near you.

- If you change your mind about what you're trying to prove, then you have to change your conclusion.

- State your conclusion strongly so that there's absolutely no doubt about your point of view.

✍ THINGS TO DO

1. Say something about these conclusions from student essays. Do they fit the requirements of the key points in this section?

   a) An impaired driver has little or no respect for life, including his own. It makes sense to come down hard on him when he is found to be impaired for the first time. As it is, our judicial system allows the offender a second opportunity to cause a serious accident, since the initial penalty is no more than a scare tactic. We need to change this system to stop such a driver before he ever has a chance to cause injury or death. Making the first penalty a harsh one would pressure all drivers to think and stay alive rather than drink and drive.

   b) While the man himself was not immortal, what his life's work stood for certainly was. Up to the moment of his death, Martin Luther King Jr. was doing the memorable things he did every day of his life. His devotion to inspiring and helping his people has made him a powerful symbol not only for his time, but for ours as well.

   c) As it stands, television's capacity as a tool for learning has been overlooked by most networks in favour of action and sensationalism. It is true that some stations are showing educational programs that work as correspondence courses and that these programs are largely interactive ones. But, by itself, this one area is simply not enough. Television as a means of learning may be improving slowly, but it still has a long way to go.

2. Look at an essay you're working on now. Do you know what you're trying to prove? Write down in a sentence what your conclusion is.

3. Take a look at a friend's essay. Ask your friend to tell you what the conclusion is. Ask her if she's clear about what she's trying to prove.

4. Look back to the essays at the end of Chapter 1 (pages 17–19). What is each one trying to prove? Write out the conclusion of each one in a sentence.

5. Read an article in a newspaper or a magazine. Does the conclusion say what the answer is? Does the introduction suggest what the answer is?

6. Make up essay topics (formulate some questions) and then think of some one-sentence answers that could be developed into essays.

7. Work in groups in class to formulate and answer essay topics with one-sentence answers. Then take one or two of your group's answers and give reasons for them.

THE BODY

It's now time to go back through the information and thinking that led you to your conclusion and present this information and thinking to your reader in the clearest way possible. It's time to move from thinking about what you're trying to prove to thinking about the best way to prove it. It's time to move from the conclusion to the body.

1. Conclusion

2. Body

 SPOT CHECK

Whether on an informal or a formal level, you've done an amount of reading, listening, viewing, and talking in relation to your topic. In either case, you've probably encountered a considerable load of material — most of it interesting, but much of it unnecessary for what you're trying to prove. You've also done a significant amount of thinking about your topic, but, again, much of it may not be helpful for what you're doing. What *do* you do, then, with the information and the thoughts that you don't need?

Well, you simply leave them out. They may have been trivial items or "dead ends" that were interesting but that led nowhere. So for your special purpose in that essay, you don't need to reproduce them for your reader. Tom, for instance, may have discovered Mick Jagger's age or Charlie Watts's favourite colour. But it's clear that neither of these facts was important in the proof he gave Tina for his view of The Rolling Stones, so he simply left them out.

If you don't need to use all the points that led you to your conclusion, which ones *do* you include? You include the ones that are *the most important to your conclusion*, the ones that most clearly will persuade your reader. When Tina asked Tom his reasons for his view, he gave what he thought were the most convincing ones. They had to be the most convincing reasons for him because they were the ones he based his view on. Consequently, they were the ones he chose to convince Tina (and, later, the readers of his essay). Tom chose what was important for his viewpoint and left out everything else.

Sometimes, though, this is hard to do. It may be difficult to decide which material should be included and which should be omitted. But, if you're clear about your conclusion — the direction in which you're taking your reader — you'll be able to decide which is the best proof or evidence to support that view. Remember, too, that if at some point you change your conclusion, you'll also have to change the proof or the body of the essay.

The material you retain to convince your reader of your point of view, then, makes up the body of the essay. It's this material on which you base the evidence, the facts, the proof for your conclusion. What, then, do you do with this material?

★ KEY POINTS

1. Choose only your best points to support your conclusion. The number of points you select will depend on how many you need to support your conclusion convincingly and how long the essay is. Tom and the writers of the student essays that you've looked at have used three points to support their views in their short (approximately 300-word) essays. For longer essays you'd use either more points or develop the two or three most important ones by writing more about each.

2. When you have the points you need, you'll have to arrange them in the best possible order. This usually means starting off with

the minimum-strength points, moving to medium-strength ones, and ending with the strongest. While all your points are strong ones — remember, you've chosen only the best ones to convince your readers — some will just naturally appear stronger than others. The reason for this progression is that the strongest are needed at the end to clinch your argument, to cause your reader to reach the same conclusion that you yourself have reached. The effect of arranging the points in this way is the same as the effect of finding the strongest point at the climactic part of a song, book, film, or dance. "Saving the best for last" is a sure way of driving home your strongest point with the greatest impact. In his essay, for example, Tom put what he thought was his strongest point (the one that carried the most statistical weight) right before the conclusion.

3. Arrange your points logically. If one point *needs* to come before another, then you must make sure that it does. This is like saying that "A" must lead to "B," "B" must lead to "C," "C" must lead to "D," and so on. If you were trying to persuade your reader of the logic of the sequence of events involved in learning to drive a car, for instance, it would make more sense to discuss something basic, like starting the car and putting it into motion, *before* you deal with an advanced operation, such as parallel parking. In other cases, however, such as in Tom's essay, where the points may not be connected logically, there's no need to try to relate them in this way.

4. Use your main points and your conclusion to create an outline, the same way you did with Tom's points (pages 10–11). An outline will give you a clear picture at any given time of what your answer is and what reasons you're using to support it. Keep the outline as a guide to your approach in any particular essay and as a reminder of your reasons when you come to announce them in the introduction.

☼ HIGHLIGHTS

- Omit unnecessary points and keep only the most relevant.

- According to the length and detail required for the essay, decide how many points you'll need and how much each one should be developed.

- Use your main points to create an outline.

- If you change your conclusion, change your points and outline.

- Arrange your points from minimum-strength to strongest.

- Arrange your points in a logical order.

✐ THINGS TO DO

1. Create an outline with a conclusion and three points to back it up for each of the following topics:

   a) Is hitchhiking a good way to travel?

   b) Do students have rights?

   c) Why aren't there more female professional athletes?

   d) What are the best features of your province?

   e) Is saving money important?

   f) Does it matter if Elvis is alive?

   g) Are today's families having more trouble staying together?

   h) What's good about soap operas?

2. Look at an essay that you're working on now. How many points have you used to support the conclusion? Have you kept only the best ones? How are your points connected? Do they go from minimum-strength to strongest? Are they in a logical order?

3. Complete the same process as in question 2 with a friend's essay.

4. Look back to the essays at the end of Chapter 1 (pages 17–19). What points do these students use to back up their conclusions? What order are they in? What other points might they have used?

5. Look at the newspaper or magazine article you used to answer question 5 at the end of "The Conclusion" (page 27). What points are used to back up the conclusion in that article? Are they the best ones? What order are they in?

6. Think of some points to develop your one-sentence answers to question 6 at the end of "The Conclusion" (page 28). How would you deal with them?

7. Look back at your group's points for some of your answers to essay topics in question 7 at the end of "The Conclusion" (page 28). Discuss the best order to put them in.

THE INTRODUCTION

Once you know what you're trying to prove and once you know what proof you need, you're finally ready to tell your reader what you want to say. In other words, you're ready to write the introduction. While it may seem odd to deal last with the part the reader encounters first, think about your view of an essay as an answer. It's only by knowing what your answer is (by knowing what your conclusion will be) that you can safely announce to your reader the direction in which you're heading.

2. Body

3. Introduction

Consider the alternative. If you try to start with your introduction *before* you know what you're trying to prove or before you've thought out your main supporting points, then the danger is that your essay could go anywhere — anywhere but where you want it to go.

 SPOT CHECK

Let's look back at Tom's essay. Before he wrote his introduction, he had to figure out two things: (1) the answer to Tina's question

"Which is the most popular rock group?" and (2) the reasons for his answer. Once he knew these two things — which were really the conclusion and the body of his essay — he could then announce to his readers what he was trying to prove. He could then say to his readers: "Look, I've thought about this topic. This is the way I see it. These are my reasons for seeing it this way. Can I interest you in reading about my view?" Neither Tom nor you would actually put the introduction in these words, but they convey the suggestion of what you're doing — but only once you've figured it out for yourself.

Once you know the conclusion and body of your essay, then you can use the introduction for a specific purpose: to signal to the reader the direction you're going with your topic. When you do this, the introduction becomes a *signpost* for the reader, something that tells that person what you're writing about and in what direction your main points will lead.

By telling the reader what your essay is about in the introduction, you're doing very much the same thing you're doing in the conclusion — telling what the essay is about. Think about it. In Tom's essay, the introduction tells the reader that "of all rock groups, The Rolling Stones are the most popular," and the conclusion states that "The Rolling Stones are indeed the most popular rock group." The gist of both of these assertions is the same.

But how can this be? Aren't the introduction and the conclusion two different things? Well, it's true that they're different in tone (in the way they state the answer). But, *in the fact that they both state the answer, they're really the same.* In the conclusion, *after* presenting your evidence and facts, you are stating strongly what your answer is. In the introduction, while suggesting your view, you are also stating what your answer is.

The conclusion has to be stated strongly: that's where you're driving home your answer after having given solid evidence for it. At the beginning, though, your conviction about your answer should be expressed differently from how you wrap it up. That doesn't mean you should be weak or tentative in your introduction. What it means is that you need to find a way to "hook" or intrigue your reader with what you have to say.

Readers can always make the choice not to read. Even though you may think that your teacher or professor has no choice in the matter — that he or she has to read your essay — it's still up to you to intrigue your reader to follow you further in your line of thought. For example, you probably wouldn't listen for long to someone who is dull or indecisive in a conversation, or read something that didn't make an effort to catch your interest. Similarly, while your teacher has to read your work, there's no guarantee that he or she will like reading it. What can you do, then, to get someone to want to read your essay?

★ KEY POINTS

1. Come right out and say it: make your introduction a direct statement of your answer. While this "flat-out" approach to saying something isn't very sophisticated, it does have the advantage of being clear. Using this approach, Tom could have opened his essay in a blunt way by giving only his answer and main points: "The Rolling Stones are the most popular rock band in history because _____ , _____ , and _____ ." While one sentence isn't a paragraph, this kind of approach can help you as a writer for two reasons: (1) your reader knows exactly what your answer is and (2) you have a good starting point from which to develop your ability to write more sophisticated introductions.

2. Use an "attention-grabber" to hook your reader. This approach could be as simple as using a statement, fact, or statistic to jolt your reader's interest. Using this approach, Tom might have written the following introduction: "The Rolling Stones should be dead by now. They've been hit by everything from riots at Altamont, to over-zealous fans, to years of hard-core drug use. Instead, they've survived to become the most popular rock band over the past 30 years." The shock effect of such an opening should be enough to get a reader to continue.

3. Use some interesting background information relevant to your answer. This approach shows your reader how your answer fits into the "big picture" of the issue you're addressing. Tom chooses this particular tactic by establishing for his readers a historical context for The Stones' popularity by (1) comparing them to the many vanished rock bands over the years and (2) giving an example of an early song and their most recent tour to show the span of their popularity in years.

4. Don't forget to give your answer and main points in the introduction. Your opening paragraph must state what you're trying to prove. Telling your reader right away doesn't mean giving away your big secret that you think should be saved for the end; on the contrary, if your reader doesn't know what the answer is, he or she might well wonder what the essay is about and where it's heading. This situation would be the same as seeing a movie that shows scenes and plots from three different movies. You'd certainly be at a loss to say what kind of movie you were watching and what it's about. Look back at the last sentence in Tom's introductory paragraph (pages 12–13) to see how clear he is about his answer and main points.

☼ HIGHLIGHTS

- The introduction is essentially the same as the conclusion in the sense that both tell the reader what your answer is.

- The only way they really differ is in tone: the conclusion is stated strongly, while the introduction arouses curiosity.

- You write the introduction last because it's only after you know what your answer is and what you need to prove it that you can announce it to your reader.

- The introduction is a signpost for your reader that shows the direction your essay will take.

- Use a direct statement of your answer, an "attention-grabber," or interesting background information to get your reader to pay attention to what you have to say.

- Don't forget to include your answer and main points in the introduction.

THINGS TO DO

1. Discuss these introductions to student essays. Say something about which approach each one uses, and identify each answer and its main points.

   a) Time is an aspect of life that we all share. We talk about how little we have when we want to accomplish something or how quickly time passes when we try. And yet there are those special people who seem to accomplish so much in so little time. If I could turn back the hands of time, I would want to meet Martin Luther King Jr. because he was an inspirational speaker, a courageous individual, and a great humanitarian.

   b) There should be stiffer penalties for drunk drivers in order to reduce the number of accidents, to protect drunk drivers from themselves, and to protect innocent victims.

   c) TV violence is here to stay. In fact, it has been clearly increasing over the years. Studies show that the average number of violent acts in television programming has grown in the past decade. Whether we like this trend or not, we seem to co-operate with the TV producers, who show violent acts because viewer tolerance of violent programs has increased as well.

2. Look at an essay that you're working on now. Is your introduction essentially the same as your conclusion? Do both tell the reader what the answer is? Is the introduction different in tone? Did you write your introduction last? Does it act as a signpost for your reader?

3. Do the same as in question 2 with a friend's essay. Can your friend answer these questions about the introduction?

4. Look back to the essays at the end of Chapter 1 (pages 17–19). How do these writers handle their introductions? Do they pay attention to the things we're concerned about in question 2 here?

5. Look at the article you used to answer question 5 at the end of "The Conclusion" (page 27). How is the introduction dealt with? Does it answer the concerns brought up in question 2 here?

6. Sketch out an introduction for your conclusion and points to question 6 at the end of "The Conclusion" (page 28). How would you deal with it to make it work for you?

7. As a group, write an introduction for the points and conclusion you have for question 7 at the end of "The Conclusion" (page 28).

WHAT ALL THIS ADDS UP TO

When you see the process of writing an essay in terms of answering a question, you see that there is a remarkable wholeness about the entire essay. That is, all the parts — the conclusion, the body, and the introduction — are actually just elements of the same thing: the answer. The conclusion states the answer, the body supports it, and the introduction announces it.

The benefit here is this: if you understand the parts of an essay in this way then it follows that they cannot be unrelated to each other (as in "the mechanical view") or simply be just words on a page (as in "the empty vessel view"). Connected in purpose as they are, the three parts of an essay work together in a natural and complementary way in the same sense that a person's legs, arms, and head all serve different functions yet work together for a happy result.

A HANDY LIST SHOWING THE PARTS OF AN ESSAY

Use this list as a convenient summary of the points you've looked at:

1. CONCLUSION

- Write the conclusion first, after you do your research and form a view of the topic.
- The conclusion is the essence of your answer: "what I'm trying to prove to my reader."

- To keep your focus, write the conclusion in one sentence as a reminder and refer to it to avoid going off topic.
- If you change your view of the topic, you have to change your conclusion.
- State your conclusion strongly.
- Using your conclusion as your starting point, "backtrack" to write the body.

2. BODY

- Write the body by looking back to what led you to your conclusion.
- Omit unnecessary points and keep only the most relevant.
- The number and depth of points will vary according to the length of the essay.
- Use your main points to create an outline.
- Arrange the points from minimum-strength to strongest.
- Where possible, arrange the points logically from A→ B→ C→ D.
- If you change your conclusion, change your points.

3. INTRODUCTION

- Write the introduction last, because you need to know your conclusion before you can announce it.
- The introduction is basically the same as the conclusion, because both tell what the answer is.
- The introduction differs from the conclusion in tone; the conclusion is stated strongly, while the introduction captures the reader's interest.
- The introduction is a signpost for the reader.
- Use direct statement of your answer, an "attention-grabber," or interesting background information to get your reader to pay attention.
- Include your answer and your main points in the introduction.

THE COURT CASE

Now that you've seen what an essay is and how it works, let's take a look at an example from the world of the courtroom to show the process you've just looked at. By comparing the way in which a lawyer presents her case to the way you've just thought about an essay, you should become even clearer about what you're doing. Let's understand, though, that this example probably owes more to episodes of

L.A. Law and reruns of *Perry Mason* than it does to the real world of the law, but, for our purposes, it will serve just fine.

The case concerns Kristy Kleer, who has been accused of murdering her husband, Matty Murk (Kristy had kept her own surname). Matty was found shot to death, and, after an investigation, the police arrested Kristy (they had no other suspects) and charged her with his murder. Kristy hired a lawyer, Lisa Leegull, to defend her, and for the past six months Lisa has been preparing her case.

Today is the start of the trial (which will probably go on for a few weeks), and everyone is in court looking serious and hopeful. Lisa has done a lot of work preparing her defence, and she now approaches the jury with her view of her client's position: "Ladies and gentlemen of the jury, my name is Lisa Leegull, and I am the attorney for Mrs. Kristy Kleer, who has been accused of the murder of her husband, Mr. Matty Murk. It is my view, however, that my client has been wrongfully charged, and that she is not guilty. I will, therefore, use the next few weeks of the trial to show you the facts and evidence that led me to this view, and it is my hope that they will convince you as well that Mrs. Kleer is not guilty."

What has Lisa just given the jury? Well, it seems that she's just given them the introduction. In her introduction, she's announced to the jury what her answer is — "My client is not guilty" — and in doing so shows how the introduction is the same as her conclusion. She's also fulfilled another function of the introduction by using her answer as a signpost so that the jury will know in which direction she's leading them. At the same time, though, she's announced her intention in a way that is direct, yet which sets her answer in the context of necessary background information. (Her opening sentence says that, in the overall issue of this murder case and, specifically to the accusation of guilt, Lisa's answer is "not guilty.") As well, Lisa "wrote," or prepared, her introduction last. She had to because it was only after she herself had reviewed the case and become convinced that her client was not guilty (only after all this) that she could stand in front of others to announce her introduction.

You can see, then, that all the ingredients you've considered for the introduction apply to this example. It's as though this part of Lisa's court presentation is the beginning of her "essay to the jury" and that what she's doing is verbalizing what she might otherwise have written for them.

Let's continue. Over the next few weeks of the trial, Lisa presents all kinds of facts, evidence, and proof to show that her client did not commit the murder. She notes first, for instance, that Kristy is a person who "couldn't harm a fly." She then has several people testify as to the kind, generous, and loving woman Kristy is. Kristy's neighbour, Mr. Willy Watcher, takes the stand and swears that Kristy would always be up at the crack of dawn to cut the lawn, shovel the snow, or take the children to their early morning lessons. Similarly, the housekeeper, Ms. E. Fishent, professes that "surely a woman like Mrs. Kleer couldn't have done it — she's just too nice. She would always iron his shirts herself because she knew just how he liked the creases in the sleeves, and she'd just as often prepare his favourite meal of macaroni and cheese herself than let me make it."

Lisa then moves from these testimonies about Kristy Kleer's character to Kristy's own testimony about the murder weapon itself. She shows, for example, that Kristy didn't own a gun, had never owned a gun, didn't know how to use a gun, and would even faint at the sight of a gun (and, indeed, Kristy did somewhat pale when the gun was shown to her in court). Lisa also reveals that the gun in question was not registered either to Kristy or to her husband and that Kristy's fingerprints had not been found on the gun; thus, the burden of proof falls to the prosecution to make the connection between Kristy and the murder weapon.

The third level of testimony produced an eyewitness who helped confirm Kristy's testimony as to her whereabouts at the time of the alleged murder: namely, that she had been out of town that particular weekend visiting a close friend, Mrs. Otto Town. Mrs. Town, a famous brain surgeon, supported Kristy's story that the two of them had spent the entire weekend together shopping, and said that it was absolutely impossible for Kristy to have been in two places — the shopping mall and the murder scene — at the same time.

All right, let's stop to consider what has happened here. Lisa has just presented the jury with evidence for her answer, her point of view. She's just given the jury a look at the things that led her to the conclusion that her client is not guilty. In other words, she's presented the body of her "essay" on the topic *The Defence of Kristy Kleer*.

How well has she shaped the points she's presented? Well, she's certainly left out all the unnecessary ones that came to her in her own investigation of the details (some of which may have been interesting or even helpful but which were less relevant than the points she chose for the jury). The points she finally chose were the result of the formal research that led her to the conclusion that Kristy was not guilty, and she "backtracked" through that research when it came to constructing the body. She decided on the number of points she'd need to make her case convincing and arranged them in the best possible order. Note how she began with her minimum-strength point (testimony about Kristy's character), moved to a medium-strength one (the lack of connection between Kristy and the murder weapon), and ended with the strongest (an important eyewitness account of Kristy's whereabouts at the time of the murder). If Lisa presents these points reasonably and well, she's doing the most she can in the body of this "essay" to bring the jury to her conclusion: that Kristy is not guilty.

Finally, after all the evidence has been given, Lisa approaches the jury at the end of the trial and says: "Ladies and gentlemen of the jury, I have taken these past few weeks to convince you of what I am already convinced: namely, that my client, Mrs. Kristy Kleer, is not guilty of the murder of her husband. I have presented you with facts, testimony, and evidence to bring you around to share my view about my client. It is now time for you to make a decision. Can you possibly say, beyond a shadow of a doubt, that Mrs. Kleer, a caring mother and wife, could have been capable of the crime of which she stands accused? Now that you have heard about Mrs. Kleer, a woman who cares about her family and husband, a woman who knows nothing about guns, a woman who was not even at the scene of the crime, I urge you to search your hearts and minds and find the only reasonable verdict: that Kristy Kleer is not guilty of the murder of her husband."

It should be clear that Lisa has reached her conclusion: she has provided the answer that Kristy Kleer is not guilty. As well, she has fulfilled the other requirements of the conclusion: (1) she arrived at it through the research that she did on the case; (2) she had her conclusion down before she "backtracked" to form the body and the introduction; (3) she stated her conclusion in one (her last) sentence; (4) she stated it strongly so that there can be no doubt about her point of view; and (5) she built her case in such a way that, if she changed her mind about her conclusion, she could change the body and the introduction to fit her new answer.

The parallels between Lisa's courtroom presentation and writing an essay are quite strong. You can see clear similarities between the way she sets out to convince the jury of Kristy's innocence and the things you have to do when you write an essay. Keep "the court case" in mind and refer to it whenever you're stuck writing an essay.

Finally, just how well Lisa achieved what she set out to do is entirely up to the jury, who in this case serve as the "readers" of her "essay" on *The Defence of Kristy Kleer*. In a way, the jury will "mark" her presentation with their verdict of "guilty" or "not guilty." In a similar way, the readers of your essays — your teachers and professors — will mark how well you have presented your thinking on a topic, on how well you have shown them that you know what an essay is.

FOUR ADVANTAGES OF THE COMMON SENSE APPROACH

When you begin to think of essay writing as a common sense process, you'll see that there are four distinct advantages to this approach.

1. AN ESSAY *IS* INTEGRATED

This means that all the parts of an essay — the conclusion, the body, and the introduction — are parts of the same thing: your answer. They grow naturally out of your answer, and if you think about them and develop them in the way you've seen, they are all integrated with and connected to each other. The advantage of this point is that now there is little chance that you'll go off track from your purpose and end up shifting topic or writing two essays.

2. AN ESSAY *IS* FLEXIBLE

This means that your essay can change to be either a long or a short response to the essay question. If you know what your answer is, then you can respond with a short essay (one to three pages) or a longer one (five to ten pages or more). If you wanted to, you could even write a book on your topic. In all cases your answer stays the same; the only thing you need to do to make your essay longer is more research and thinking. If you're clear about what your answer is, the length of the essay depends on how little or how much you want to say about it. The advantage of this point is that your thinking isn't determined by length. Instead, your thinking determines the length of the essay.

3. AN ESSAY *IS* CHANGEABLE

This means that you can change your mind about your answer, about what you're trying to prove. If you're writing the body based on the conclusion you've reached and then decide that you really want to prove a different conclusion, just write out your new conclusion and go back to change the body to support it. In some cases, if the new conclusion is only slightly different, you'll probably still be able to use most of the evidence you had from your first essay. The advantage of this point is that you're not locked into any particular conclusion; if your answer changes, your essay can change just as easily.

4. AN ESSAY *IS* KNOWABLE

This means that what you do when you write an essay is really what you do with your thinking all the time: you arrive at a conclusion based on some research and then present both the conclusion and research to other people for their comments. Since you do this all the time anyway, there's no reason you can't repeat the same process when you write an essay.

These four advantages show something important: that writing an essay is not a rigid, static, abstract concept but rather a flexible, dynamic, common sense process that everyone is quite familiar with and good at. Each essay you write only asks you to repeat the thought process you go through every day in order to arrive at your ideas about things. True, when you write an essay you have to do a few things a bit differently — such as formal research and writing down your thoughts on paper — but the process you go through to form your ideas and present them to your readers is one that you already know well.

So, if this process is one that you do well anyway, then there's no reason you shouldn't be able to use it to write good essays. Because now there's every reason that *you* should be able to do what your teachers can do — see an essay as precise (a specific answer), structured (developing in a logical order), and unified (all the parts relating to each other).

CHAPTER 3

USING YOUR NEW UNDERSTANDING OF AN ESSAY

WHY YOU WRITE

All right, you've looked at what an essay is and you now understand how it works. You also have a good sense of how looking at an essay in this way can help you. Now it's time to move on to think about how to use this understanding and its advantages.

Before taking that step "forward," though, this is a good time to take one "back" and to put essay writing into some sort of perspective. A good reason to do so is that it's one thing to suggest *how* to do something, but it's also valuable to think about *why* you do it. People can tell you what to do or even how to do it (like write an essay), and you may even be able to do it quite well, but the whole thing makes much more sense when you know why you're doing it — when you know what it means to you. So let's think about some of the reasons why you write essays. And let's start by thinking about some of the reasons why you write anything at all.

When you dig into the issue of "why you write," you soon see that there are only two kinds of writing you really ever do. One is writing that you *want* to do. The second is writing that you *have* to do. Let's take a look at these one at a time.

What kind of writing would you *want* to do? Try to think of some examples. Most of the things that you'll probably think of could be called "recreational" writing or "leisure" writing. These are types of writing that you might do for fun because you enjoy doing them. What are they? Well, you might have thought of keeping a diary or journal, or of writing a note, or letter, or postcard.

But do you do this kind of writing anymore? Do you keep a diary, send postcards, or write letters? While you may want to, for the most part, you either don't do them or you find ways to get around doing them. For one thing, technology makes it easy for you to get around writing to someone because most of the time you can simply use the phone to get in touch. For another, keeping a diary or journal requires some discipline and regularity and if you don't keep at it on a daily basis it's easy to lose interest. Even though there are types of writing that you may want to do and may even enjoy, it's not always easy to keep them up when you might be tempted to take shortcuts or not keep at them.

As a result, there isn't much writing that you may want to do. Knowing this becomes important when you come to think about the second category: writing that you *have* to do. Writing that you have to do is usually writing that you encounter in your life as a student or worker; you have to write in school, college, university, or in whatever job you do. These are the times and places that you have to write, and you have to because your teachers, professors, instructors, bosses, supervisors, or colleagues ask you to express your thoughts to them on paper.

This is where essay writing comes in. While there are other types of writing that you have to do — such as memos, business letters, reports, summaries, logs, prospectuses, journals — writing essays is probably the most common form of writing that you have to do in school. Think of the number of courses for which you have to write essays: marketing courses, arts courses, nursing courses, science courses, psychology courses, English courses, to name just a few. Every one of these courses requires you to respond to the ideas and material in that course by writing an essay about what has been discussed.

It's here that the connection between *wanting* to write and *having* to write comes in. Since there may not be much writing that you do outside of school, you can often have difficulty with the writing that you have to do in school. If you haven't had much desire to or encouragement to write, you'll have had little chance to develop either the skills or enthusiasm that you need to cope with the writing that you have to do in school. Consequently, when you get to college or university and a teacher gives out an essay assignment, the outcome isn't always the happy one that's expected by either you or your teacher. It should come as no surprise, really, that if you don't feel comfortable or familiar with writing in the first place, you will also feel uncomfortable or unfamiliar with a highly specialized form of writing: essay writing.

Yet, if you don't feel comfortable with writing, there's another form of communication that you probably do feel comfortable with — and that's *talking.* You've likely more than once said this to a teacher: "Why should I *write* this essay? Let me *tell* you about it instead." And when you do tell about it, you're very good. You're probably very articulate, enthusiastic, and knowledgeable when you're talking about an essay, when you're giving a *spoken* instead of a *written* response.

But this shouldn't be too surprising. You've seen that there's not much need for you to write when you don't want to. You should also be able to see that the world in which everyday communication occurs these days is mostly an oral and aural one: that is, speaking and hearing, rather than reading or writing. The communication that comes to you through radio and television is, in a sense, "easy" communication — you just passively "take in" what you see and hear.

One beneficial result of listening to so much, though, is that you develop a good "ear" for language. And because you continually *hear* language being used, you become good at *speaking* it. So it shouldn't be a surprise that you can speak well on a topic or that you would prefer to talk to a teacher about an essay rather than write about it. Speaking is your strong point — it's something that you're better at than writing.

If you're a better speaker than you are a writer, how can you use your ability to speak well to help yourself become a better writer? And what about writing essays? Why should you want to sit through the "torture" of learning to write essays when you can't see how learning to write essays is of any value to you? Well, the following points suggest some answers to these questions.

★ KEY POINTS

1. Since you often speak about a topic better than you write about it, *you should use your speaking skills to help yourself when you have to write something.* You can do this in several ways: You can record your ideas about a topic into a tape recorder; then play the tape back, hear yourself "talking out" your ideas, and write down what you've said as a starting point for your essay. "Talk out" your ideas to yourself and take notes as you talk. "Talk out" your views to a friend or class-mate, in much the same way that Tom talked about his view of The Rolling Stones to Tina. In these ways, you can use your speaking skills to work out your ideas on paper; the more you can connect your writing to the way you communicate the best — talking — the more you can build your ability to write.

2. Try to understand *why* you are asked to write essays in the first place. Contrary to popular belief, essay writing was not created by teachers as a form of punishment or "mental cru-elty." *The only thing that essay writing gives you is a chance for you and your teacher to look at your thoughts.* No one can actually look into your head to see what's going on there. However, by "capturing" your thinking on paper (the same as you might do with a series of snapshots if you could photo-graph thinking), both you and your teacher are able to look at your ideas, — how you've developed them, what order you've put them in — to see how you both can evaluate and improve your ability to think things out.

3. Try to see the value of essay writing in terms of your career or business goals. Essay writing can do two things: (a) it can make you a better thinker and (b) it can make you more articulate (better able to express yourself). If I'm an employer and I'm looking to hire someone for a job, who would I choose? Well, the person who gets the job will obviously have to have both knowledge of and experience in that field. Then let's say I've got two applicants who have the same degree of knowledge and experience. Which one would I choose? Well, probably the one who is more articulate and a better thinker. Consequently, the person who has "the whole package" — the one who has the required knowledge, experience, and who can write essays — is the one who gets the job. It's as simple as that. Looking at it another way, it's hardly a coincidence that many people who go to law school first get a degree in English, history, or any other area of study in which they had to write a lot of essays.

4. As much as essay writing can help you in your career, it can also help you in your everyday life. Because essay writing helps you become more articulate and a better thinker, you can also use these skills on a daily basis to become a better advocate. Advocacy means "representing someone" or "acting on behalf of" a person or group. Being an advocate isn't as uncommon an activity as it may sound. In fact, you're an advocate for someone or something all the time. When a person steps in front of you in a lineup, when your bank account is overdrawn, when you march to protest increased tuition fees, you're explaining yourself or representing your viewpoint. As well, you advocate not just for different reasons, but for different people: yourself, a friend or relative, or a social or community group. Tom, for example, is an advocate of The Rolling Stones to Tina, while Lisa is an advocate on behalf of Kristy Kleer to the judge and the jury. In the same way, the benefits of becoming a better writer make you a better advocate.

☼ HIGHLIGHTS

- If you're having difficulty writing out your ideas about something, use your speaking skills to help you out.

- Learn to see essay writing as a means to improve your ability to think and express yourself.

- Writing essays well will give you an advantage when you apply for a job and when you're in line for promotion.

- Essay writing can also benefit your personal life since it helps you become a better advocate.

✍ THINGS TO DO

Do these activities at home or with another student in class:

1. Besides the examples used in this book, think of some other kinds of writing you normally do. Which of these do you *want to do*? Which of these do you *have to do*? How do you feel about doing either kind?

2. Think about how you express yourself when speaking and when writing. Do you see any difference in your abilities in these areas? Which are you more comfortable with? Think of some other ways to use your speaking skills to help you when you have to write.

3. Make an appointment to interview someone in your career field. Ask this person about her or his attitude to writing. Ask questions such as: What kind of writing do you usually do in your job? Do you think that writing is important to you in your job? Has your attitude to writing changed since you started your job? How do you feel about what you have to write? Are you comfortable with and confident about your abilities as a writer? How important is your writing to other people at work, such as your boss, your co-workers, your employees? How do you view

your writing ability in terms of your chances for promotion? Discuss the results of your interview in class.

4. Make an appointment to interview someone who writes for a newspaper or magazine. Ask the same questions as in question 3. Discuss your answers.

5. Interview a member of an advocacy group. This can be any charitable group, volunteer agency, political association, tenants' group, or community group (for example, a humane society, a community centre, a food bank, a political office, a government agency). Ask the kinds of questions you asked in question 3, but also include the following ones: What kinds of skills have you acquired from learning to write well? Have these skills helped you become a better advocate for yourself on an everyday level? How? Have these skills helped you become a better advocate for the people you represent in your group? How? Discuss these answers in class.

FINDING YOUR TOPIC

Now that you've thought about *why* you write, let's go back to thinking about *how* you write. Remember that you've come to see an essay as an answer to a question. Remember, too, that the "question" you're answering is really your essay topic. As a student who has to respond to an essay topic, the first thing you have to ask yourself is, "Where is this topic coming from?"

When you think about it, you soon see that the topic can come from only two places. The topic can come from "inside" — that is, you yourself have to come up with the idea, shape it, and express it. The topic can also come from "outside" — in this case, your instructor has to come up with it and articulate it. Inside or outside — there are no other choices. Either you think of it or someone else does. Let's look at these sources for topics and see how best to handle each one.

If you had to choose a topic to write about, what kind of topic would it be? Well, you'd probably choose something that you like to write about. If you have any choice in a situation you usually do things that you like. When you have to choose something to write about, then, your choice will usually be something you're interested in.

That doesn't mean you can't write about something you don't like or something that you're not interested in. Sometimes you might find yourself doing just that. For example, if you don't smoke and don't like it when other people smoke, you may find yourself wanting to write about why people want to smoke or why they find it necessary to smoke. Most of the time, though, you'll probably choose a topic that you like when you have to write an essay and when the choice of topic is yours.

But it might not be enough simply to think of a topic that interests you, especially when you're writing on a topic that's related to the subject matter you're studying in a course. What do you do then? Well, in that case, you'll want to come up with a topic that is *both interesting to you* and *relevant to your course material.* This situation can be more challenging than just thinking of a topic that interests you.

Yet it makes sense for two reasons. For one, you're the person taking that course, so it's your responsibility to learn what you can from it. This means doing research, reading textbooks and articles, listening to the instructor's lectures, and taking part in class discussions. Taken together, these activities make up the part you play in your own learning. Writing an essay and coming up with a relevant topic are also important parts of your "job" as a student. The other reason why your choice of topic should be relevant is this: your instructor will be able to learn something about you and your ability to deal with the material through your choice of topic. He or she will be able to learn about your area of interest and how much you are "in tune" with the material. So choosing well is important because it helps both you and your instructor.

But it's also hard work. You've probably thought that you'd prefer to choose your own topic rather than respond to something assigned to you. You might have said, "If only *I* could choose my own topic...." or "I'd rather pick my own topic than have to write about something I'm not interested in." But many times this situation creates its own difficulties.

And the biggest of these is this: in order to create your own essay topic, you'd have to know quite a lot about that subject area. You'd have to research your subject thoroughly to find out all you can about it in order to come up with a relevant and specific essay topic. Let's look at this kind of situation.

🔖 SPOT CHECK

Say you're in a course and one of the areas your class is studying is the media. You decide that "television" would be a relevant and interesting topic to write about. Then you start to wonder, "How many things could I ask about 'television'?" And the obvious answer soon comes to you: "Quite a few." So what do you do next?

Well, in terms of general knowledge, as a long-time TV watcher, you may think that your first-hand knowledge of television might be sufficient for you to think of a topic. But in order to come up with something relevant and specific, you decide to research the subject. You certainly know what a television is and you may know of some TV shows — especially your favourite ones — but you soon see that thinking about television is different from watching it.

And when you find out more and more about television, you begin to ask yourself questions. You see that your questions start out as general ones but soon become more specific. You might start with a question like, "Does watching television harm people?" but you quickly see that this is too open-ended, too broad a question to deal with easily. It's hard to deal with such a topic when you don't know any details about "What kind of TV viewing is harmful?", "How much of it is harmful?", "Is any of it good?", or "What kind of people are affected?" These aspects are just too general, too undefined, for you to say something detailed and accurate about them.

After more thought, you soon see that a better question for an essay topic on television might be "How does watching cartoons affect children?" This is a far better choice because you now know what kind of viewing is involved (watching cartoons) and who is doing the viewing (children). You could make this topic even more specific by narrowing the audience to "children aged 3 to 6," and cartoons to *Teenage Mutant Ninja Turtles*. This kind of topic is better because, as well as being relevant to the course, it's also specific enough for your reader to make sense of.

While there's much work involved in this thinking-out process, it's well worth doing as much as possible. The more you're able to think of not only the essay but the actual essay question itself, the more it shows you and your teacher that you're able to recognize and deal with the important issues in a course. *By thinking out these issues and by responding to them in these ways, you're taking as active a part as possible in your own learning.*

This brings us to the second option in finding a topic: when the topic comes from your instructor. Because the instructor is the person most familiar with the course material, the choice of topics that she or he offers are those that are the most relevant to the course. Whether they're specific enough or the most interesting ones is, of course, for you to decide.

If you find that the choices you're given for any essay assignment aren't ones that you want to write about, don't give up hope. Make an appointment with your instructor to discuss what you can do. For instance, if you can come up with something more interesting, you might be able to write about your choice instead. Or, if you don't want to write about any of the choices you've been given and can't come up with another (but you still have a subject area that interests you), perhaps you and your instructor can arrive at a choice together.

But even here, too, it's the *thinking* that you have to do that's important. As you've seen at other times, if you think out what an essay is, you won't react to it mechanically; if you think out why you write, you'll be a better advocate. It's the same with essay topics. If you make the effort and give it some thought, you'll find one that you're happy with and learn something from having found it.

★ KEY POINTS

1. Ask yourself, "Is my essay topic relevant to this course?" There should be some logical relation between what you're studying in a particular course and what you choose to write about for that course. It only makes sense.

2. Ask yourself, "Is my essay topic specific enough for me to 'get a handle on it'?" Focus your essay topic enough so that what you're writing about (a) isn't too general for you to say something meaningful about it in the 3, 5, or 10 pages you have for your assignment or (b) isn't so specific that you end up writing about only one small part of the picture.

3. Think about the essay topic as a question. It's easier to respond to a specific question, so when a topic is expressed as a problem in a statement, make a question out of it (for example, "Adults have their own ideas about teenagers" can easily be changed to "What are adults' ideas about teenagers, and are they true?").

4. You need to have enough knowledge about your subject area before you can come up with your own essay topic, so it's up to you to get that knowledge. Both Tina and Tom had to know something about rock music in general and The Rolling Stones in particular before they could come up with a question and an answer about the popularity of rock bands. The more you know about your subject, the better you'll be able to ask questions about it. For academic courses, the best place to get information about your subject is the library, but watching films or documentaries, taking a tour, or interviewing a specialist in that field can also help.

✍ THINGS TO DO

1. It's a good idea to put your essay topic into the form of a question. Here are some topics written as statements. Can you make questions out of them?

   - The Effects of Watching Too Much Television
   - Being a Single Parent
   - Movie Stars are Over-paid
   - Taking Drugs Isn't Smart
   - Chores at Home
   - Stories in the *National Enquirer*
   - Public Transit is Necessary
   - Sex in Advertising
   - Politicians and the Public
   - A Part-Time Job

   Discuss in class whether or not these topics are specific enough. If they need to be narrowed down, work with a classmate to make them better. Compare the responses from different groups.

2. These are some courses in which you'd have to write an essay. Think of essay topics that would be relevant and specific for each.

media studies	marketing	social work
auto mechanics	psychology	sociology
career planning	English	religion
fashion design	nursing	electronics
political science	philosophy	history

3. Here are some essay topics. Point out which ones are relevant to a particular course and say something about whether they seem general or specific.

a) If you could go back in time and meet anyone from history, who would it be, and why?

b) How influential is fashion?

c) Adopted children have a right to know who their birth parents are. Do you agree or disagree?

d) Television is (or is not) harmful to learning.

e) Should there be stiffer penalties for drunk drivers?

f) Voting is a fundamental right in a democratic society.

g) Are little boys of today less chauvinistic than their fathers were as boys?

h) Your city has recently brought in a law that makes restaurants designate one-half of their seating as a non-smoking section. Most restaurant owners are angry about this legislation. What is your view?

COMING UP WITH IDEAS

So you now have an essay topic to answer. What's next? Well, when you listened to Tom and Lisa, you saw that they could come up with their answers only once they had done certain things. Only once they'd read about, heard about, seen, talked about, and thought about their area of interest could they actually *come up with ideas* about their topic and arrive at a point of view about it. And you have to do the same things in order to deal with your essay topic.

But which of these activities is the best? Well, since you are in college or university, most of your essay assignments are *formal* ones and require

that you do most of your research in the library. Reading books and articles is usually the best way of finding out information about the topic; then, you can use this information to come to your answer or conclusion. With this kind of research, you become "immersed" in or involved in the material until you become knowledgeable about it. Through learning as much as you can about the topic, you should eventually feel comfortable enough to be able to speak or write about it with a high degree of confidence.

However, your research shouldn't be limited to that method alone. You should be able to get a "fullness of knowledge" through any method you can. Let's look at some other methods as well.

 SPOT CHECK

Say that your essay assignment deals with the situation of Native peoples and that the essay topic is: "How did Native peoples arrive at their social conditions today?" This topic could have been assigned in a number of courses: sociology, history, social work, psychology, to name a few. Well, if you know only a little or nothing at all about the situation of Native peoples today or in the past, what do you do?

The obvious thing to do, of course, is to read about it. Books, magazines, and newspapers in the library can give you both historical and up-to-date information. But don't limit yourself only to those books, magazines, and newspapers written by non-Natives. A trip to a Native cultural centre, for example, would provide you with examples of work produced by Native writers or Native associations. Keep your mind open to as many sources of information as possible.

Other methods to explore include *hearing* and *seeing* various perspectives on Native situations. By going to the movies (or by renting videos) you can see and hear portrayals of Native peoples in movies such as *Little Big Man, Dances With Wolves, Black Robe,* and *Thunderheart.* These presentations may seem less "authentic" or "scholarly" than documented research in textbooks, but they can give you a visual and auditory experience of situations that books can't. Other places where you can get this kind of experience are displays of Native art, plays such as *Dry Lips Oughta Move To Kapuskasing,* and Native cultural events.

Still another thing to do is to talk to some Native Canadians. Find out directly how they see themselves and their situation. Get the names of various Native associations and make an appointment to interview someone there. This kind of connection can also provide other leads: talking to one person can put you in touch with another, and so on. Such "networking" can open up opportunities for you to gain information that, again, books themselves may not be able to give.

Whichever area you explore, though, it's a good idea to take notes and ask questions. Your notes will give you the information you need to come up with ideas, and you'll be able to look back at them as you work through an essay; the questions you ask about this information should lead you to specific points about your topic.

Finally, the result of using all of these methods is that, through exploring the topic on several levels, you can come up with as many good ideas as possible to help you arrive at your answers. Remember that reading what's in the library is a good source for information, but it's not the only one. The others mentioned above can help just as much.

You might think, though, that you can't find the time for all this research. You might say, "I can hardly find the time to read what's in the library — where will I find the time to explore these other areas?" It's a question of priorities. If you're paying for your education and if — as with other things in your life — you want "value for your money," then some of that "value" has to come from you. Your teachers can help you in the process, but no one can make you learn. That's where the effort to do the exploring comes in. And only you can say if it's worth it.

✍ THINGS TO DO

1. Take a tour of your library. You can do this with your class or simply by making an appointment with a librarian. Find out how the books, magazines, and newspapers are arranged and how to use the microfiche machine. Ask about how to use the subject index to "zero-in" on a subject area. Get to know your librarian, and visit as often as you can. These are the most helpful people you can know when you have to write an essay.

   If you take a tour with your class, discuss your impressions as soon as possible afterwards. Think about your responses to these questions:

   • Do you feel comfortable in the library?

   • Did you learn anything from the tour?

   • Did you know most of what you saw from previous visits?

   Suggest some ways in which the library can help you with your research.

2. Find out what you can about the development of comic books. Where did they start? When did they start? What were the reasons they started?

   Look in the library for whatever information you can find. Talk to friends or family members who are collectors. Go to comic-book shops and talk to the people who work there. Look in the yellow pages of the phone book for clubs or associations that deal in or trade comic books. Interview someone in a comic-book club.

PLANNING YOUR ANSWER

When you're asked to organize your ideas to support your answer, you might say to your teacher: "Can't I just tell you if I like something or not? Why do I have to bother with details?" Well, giving reasons or organizing your ideas to back up your answer isn't just "bothering with details." When you use your ideas to plan your answer, you are telling your reader *your specific reasons for your point of view.* You've done your reading, listening, viewing, talking, and thinking about your topic to come up with an answer to your essay topic and the points that led you to that answer. Now it's your job to use those points to back up your answer, to persuade your reader to agree with you.

A one-word response — a simple "yes" or "no" — just isn't enough. Consider this example. Imagine that you've got this essay topic: "Is smoking a good thing to do?" It's certainly possible to answer just "yes" or "no" to this question. But a one-word answer isn't enough to fully convince someone of your response. People will want to know more: they'll want to know *why* someone should smoke or not. Think about it. Are *you* usually convinced of something when someone gives you a one-word answer?

Suppose you want to see a certain movie and a friend of yours has already seen it. You ask your friend if you should go to see that movie and the reply is "no." Is that enough for you? Are you satisfied with that answer? Well, perhaps if you trust that person's opinion completely, you won't go. However, if you're like most people, you're somewhat sceptical. You'll want to know *why* you shouldn't go. You'll want to hear your friend's ideas, opinions, and reasons why you shouldn't see that movie. Is it too violent? Is the acting bad? What about the special effects? These are some of the specific things you would want to hear about before making your decision.

Now suppose you've just met someone that you're crazy about. One day, you ask the big question, "Do you love me?" and the answer is "yes." You're happy as can be. But can you stop there? Don't you need to know more? Don't you want to find out about details? Don't you want to know *why?* "Is it my eyes you love most?" "Is it my hair?" "My smile?" "Or is it just my bank account?" If you asked this person to write an essay in response to the topic "Do you love me?" you'd want to read about not only the answer itself (hopefully "yes"), but all the important reasons behind that answer as well. This is where planning your answer is important — *it tells you everything your reader needs to know about your answer.*

Yet giving only a one-word answer is a start. It's actually a significant step because you have to go through an exploration process and have to think about the topic to arrive at even a one-word or one-sentence answer. What sometimes happens, though, is that you don't realize you've already done this, and you aren't aware that you really know much more than you think you do.

For example, if you gave me a one-word answer to an essay topic, I'd start by asking you why you thought that was the answer. After some hesitation or "talking around" the question, you'd probably "take off" on the topic in a way that shows you've got more ideas about it than you thought you had. And, once you stopped *talking* about it, I'd ask you to start *writing* about it. Before you know it, you'd have more ideas down on paper than you could ever use.

But there's also another reason why giving a one-word or a one-sentence answer is important. It means that you've actually reached a conclusion about your topic, that you've got something to prove, that you've got an answer to the question. So your brief response isn't a "bad" thing. In fact, it's actually quite good. What it means is that you know what your essay will be about.

 SPOT CHECK

Now let's see how you can plan out an answer. Let's say that you've got the essay topic, "What does car safety mean to you?" and that you've explored the subject and have come up with a number of ideas about it. You go through the notes you've made during your research and list your main points under the topic. Your list looks like this:

Car Safety

brakes	good tires	seatbelts
insurance	positive attitude	car phone
engine tune-up	brake lights	Canadian Automobile
driver training	safety kit	Association membership

What do you see when you look at this list? Well, the first thing you may see is that some of the points don't seem to have much in common with other points. For example, what do "seatbelts" have in common with "CAA membership?" One thing is a safety device to prevent injury in an accident while the other is an association to help in a road emergency. Looking at the list more closely, though, you soon see that some points *do* have a connection with others. "Seatbelts," for instance, looks as though it can be grouped with "brake lights" and "brakes" because they are all mechanical safety features — they all prevent injury to riders in a collision.

By grouping these three features together, you can arrive at your answer to the question: "To me, car safety means having a car with mechanical safety features such as brake lights, brakes, and seatbelts." And, now that you've reached your conclusion, you can backtrack to your main points, put them in order, and write about each in a separate paragraph.

Putting your main points in this order means that you're saying to your reader: "While these are all good points, I'm starting with the minimum-strength ones and ending with the strongest. My opening point — brake lights — is important as a general warning device to other drivers; my stronger point — brakes — is more important because the brakes actually stop the car; and my strongest point — seatbelts — is the most important because they're the devices that can save my life in case of a collision."

So as you can see, grouping your points together leads you to your conclusion. Because you've grouped points that are similar to each other, you can arrive at a statement about what you're trying to prove. Grouping your points also lets you plan your answer because the points themselves give you the proof you need to back it up.

But is it possible to come up with another answer? Can you go in another direction? Well, if you look at "CAA membership" again, you see that this point can be grouped with two other points: "driver training" and "insurance." By grouping these three features, you're arriving at a different answer to the same essay topic: "To me, car safety means having contact with three important automobile companies."

Moving from this response back to the main points that led you to this conclusion says this to your reader: "I'm connecting these three points logically in the order in which I'd belong to each of them as I become a licensed and safe operator of a motor vehicle: first, I'd take driver training to become a qualified driver; second, I'd take out insurance to cover myself, my car, and other drivers and their vehicles; and, third, I'd become a member of a road emergency company."

Then you can go back to those points, develop them, and present them to your reader as proof for your conclusion.

This is how you plan out any essay. What this method gives you is an outline, or a road to take, in charting out your purpose on paper.

Remember, though, that you can change your mind. If, for example, you started by saying that car safety has more to do with mechanical features than it does with belonging to car associations and, later, after thinking about it, you decide to change your mind, you can do so. All you have to do then is to change your points as well.

Whichever response you decide to choose, remember also that you're not going to use *all* of your points. You might use more than the three you used in these examples, but, unless you're writing a very long essay, you'll rarely use them all. Don't worry if you don't. Just leave them aside.

The last important thing to consider is this: whichever answer you decide to give, one isn't necessarily better than the other — they're just different. What will make one better than the other is how well you plan your answer and how well you write it.

☼ HIGHLIGHTS

- By itself, a brief answer isn't enough to substitute for a whole essay.

- A brief answer is a good starting point, and the very fact that you have one shows that you've done more thinking about the topic than you might think.

- Planning your answer can best be done by grouping together similar points to lead you to your conclusion; then backtrack to use those points to give you the reasons for your view.

- If you want to change your answer, just look for the things that other points have in common and they should lead you to a different conclusion (if you prefer the new one, don't forget to use new points to back it up).

- Arrange your points in order.

✍ THINGS TO DO

1. Look at the topics in question 1 at the end of "Finding Your Topic" (page 54). What points can you think of for these topics? What conclusions do they lead you to?

2. Look at an article in a newspaper or magazine. Can you find the conclusion and the main points? What are they? Do they seem to be in a particular order? Discuss your findings in class.

3. Go over an essay you're working on now or one that you've got-ten back. What is your conclusion? Do your points support it? How would your essay be different if you'd chosen different points?

4. Read the following student essay. What is its conclusion? What are the points used to support it?

Clear Writing is Essential for Success

Although speech is an important and commonly used method of communication, writing is very important too. In fact, clear writing is essential for success for several reasons: one, it is a main form of communication; two, it's a very strong type of communication; and three, in some situations, your writing represents you.

Next to speaking, writing is the second most commonly used method of communication. People use some form of writing every day, whether it is writing a formal essay or simply writing out a cheque. The writing has to be clear or, quite simply, people will not understand you. To be successful in whatever you do, others must be able to comprehend whichever method of communication you choose to use, particularly with writing.

Words, especially the written word, can be very strong and mean-ingful. Writing is a concrete documentation of your thoughts, feel-ings, and ideas. If your ideas are not clearly put into writing, it can be assumed that your ideas are not clearly thought out. Success comes from clearly thought-out ideas that can be expressed in any form of communication in a comprehensible manner.

When you send a letter or memo to someone who does not know you, your writing represents you. A clearly written memo or letter can leave the reader with a clear and concise picture. This is true not only about the topic of the document but also about the person who writes it.

Whatever you write, the words you use are almost a part of you. Clear writing is never really forgotten. It is there in concrete form and can be regenerated if need be. The words of very successful people are often written down for posterity, but if they are not clearly written, the success will be short-lived.

USING DIFFERENT APPROACHES FOR YOUR ESSAY

You might have noticed that the various essays and examples in this book all have one thing in common: *they all try to get you to agree with what they have to say.* Each one takes a specific point of view and wants to *persuade* you of the "rightness" of that view by using facts and figures or points of logic. Take a moment to look back — and even forward — at some examples to see if this is true. Doesn't Tom try to convince Tina about his view of The Rolling Stones? Doesn't Lisa Leegull want the jury to believe her argument about Kristy Kleer? When you look closely and ask yourself, "What does this essay (or example) want me to do?" you'll see that it wants you to agree with it. As such, this kind of writing can be called persuasive writing. What you seek to do with your writing, then, is to convince your readers "to come on side" with the way you see things.

But this is true of communication in general. Letters, memos, junk mail, TV and radio commercials, newspaper and magazine ads, and government pamphlets all want to persuade you of one thing or another. Think about some examples: the radio commercial selling jeans, the TV show giving solutions to teen problems, the magazine ad selling a vacation, the newspaper article giving a journalist's opinion on a political party, the junk mail that wants you to buy a particular type of pizza, the government pamphlet trying to convince you to save electricity. Any of these appeals may be genuine or phony, but they're all trying to convince you of something. Even writing up a résumé and an accompanying letter for a job application is an attempt to persuade a potential employer to see you in a favourable light. You can probably think of other examples of the different kinds of writing that try to persuade.

At this point you might ask, "Is all writing persuasive or is some of it something else?" This question has a lot to do with your *purpose* when you write something. If your purpose is simply to give some information on a topic (without deliberately trying to influence your readers one way or the other), you might say that you weren't being persuasive at all. For instance, you might write a factual or objective essay that "exposes" or "reveals" something, but doesn't consciously try to persuade. Yet even in this kind of situation, you are still making decisions about what to include in your essay and what to leave out. You sift, sort, and present the information in such a way that your very arrangement of it, although it's supposedly objective, still tries to convince the reader to see something in a particular way.

Let's examine this idea a little further. If it's true that, in one way or another, all essays try to persuade someone of something, you should then ask, "Are there different ways in which you can persuade?" Well, let's look at some of the different essay types to see if they can help. Let's understand, though, that these essay types are extremely flexible. In other words, you can use any particular type to write a whole essay, or use it in only part of an essay, or even use it in combination with one or more other types in an essay. At the same time, you'll also look at how these approaches can help to develop your "essay as answer."

★ KEY POINTS

1. *Description.* In a descriptive essay, you'd want to think about the details of a person, place, or object and write them out so that your reader can see them in a certain way. For a descriptive essay, you need to ask "What does it look like?" and "How can I make my reader see it?" Remember that you're being selective in choosing these details. If you want your reader to see that person in a positive way, choose specific details to create a certain image or idea; conversely, if you want to create a negative view of that person, pick the opposite details.

   Remember, too, that you can write a whole essay using description if you need to, or you can use it only in certain places to get your reader to visualize the details. Look back to Tom's essay on The Rolling Stones and to the way in which Kristy Kleer is described by various people in "The Court Case." What specific details are being used? For what purpose? What about the "Body Image" essay in Chapter 4? Where does Jasmine use specific details to describe something? What are they? Why does she use these particular ones? Once you know what you're trying to prove in an essay, you then have to ask, "Which descriptive details will help me to prove that?" When you select those details and bring them in line with your purpose in the essay, you'll be improving your answer by giving it the description needed to convince the reader.

2. *Narration.* As you probably suspect, *narration means telling a story.* When you write a narrative essay or use narration in part of an essay, you're giving a sequence of events. You're asking yourself, "What happened?" and presenting either a whole or a part of a series of events to make a point. Of course, you're still being selective about which events you include and which you leave out, depending on your purpose in the essay.

While you can write an entire essay using narration, you're more likely to use it here and there (along with other types) to help your reader understand how the order of events is important to your points. As an example, look at the two essays on Superman in Chapter 5 and find where narration has been used to make a point. Look at how Ramesh uses one of his paragraphs to show the order of events involved in creating the comic book. Do the same in "Don't Be Afraid to Make Changes" — notice the presentation of events that occur in *Macbeth*.

Once you've decided what you're trying to prove in an essay, ask yourself how you can use narration to help you give that proof.

3. *Process.* When you use process to explain something, you're telling your reader *how something works, how to construct something, or how to do something.* You'd use process to write about how a particular sport is played, how to follow a recipe, or how the transit system in your city works. It's clear that "how" or "how to" are the operative words when you deal with this type of approach. What you're showing your reader are the steps involved in how something functions or how it's made.

As with the other essay types, you could do this for a whole essay or for only part of one. For example, look back at the conversation between Tom and Tina and identify the steps or stages that process went through. Step one would be Tom's initial response, step two would be his second and more developed response, and so on. As in the other cases, you would use process to make your case once you knew what your essay was trying to prove.

4. *Compare and contrast.* When you *compare* two or more things you're showing what's the same between them. When you *contrast* them you show what's different about them (although the word "compare" by itself can mean both compare and contrast). In this type of essay, you'd show what's the same or what's different about two related things to let your reader know what is better or worse about one or the other.

To see this approach applied to an essay, look at the two essays on *Macbeth* in Chapter 5. Each essay is a contrast to the other.

Once you know what you're trying to prove, you're then asking the natural follow-up question, "How will showing these similarities or differences help me prove my point?"

5. *Cause and effect.* As its name suggests, this type of approach *shows the cause and/or effects of something.* Note that these don't necessarily have to appear in the same essay; that is, you can write about causes in one (or use it as one approach) and effects in another.

Use this approach to show how something is caused or how something is affected — as Jasmine does in "Body Image" (Chapter 4) when she shows how society and the media cause women's attitudes about themselves to develop and how women are affected by those influences. Here, too, ask yourself how the cause-and-effect approach can help you develop your answer.

These are the most common and helpful essay types and approaches that you'd use to explain your answer. Since your essays will argue a point or try to persuade your reader, you'll probably use these types more as approaches or examples within your essay than as whole essay types themselves. But that's all right. Given that we spend so much time and effort trying to persuade others of something, it's useful to have a variety of approaches that will help you give a good answer. Don't be reluctant to choose; don't be afraid to mix and match. The examples and essays in this book often use more than one method to make a point. Take your cue from them and build on your already solid understanding of how to say it as well as you can.

☼ HIGHLIGHTS

- To some degree or other, all writing is persuasive.

- There are different essay types that can help you when you write an essay.

- Be flexible in how you use these essay types and you'll write a good essay.

✍ **THINGS TO DO**

1. Look through the essays and situations in this book. Can you find any examples of the approaches you've just looked at? Which ones are they?

2. Think of examples for each of the essay types. For instance, for cause and effect you might focus on the things that caused you to go to college or university and the effects of that decision. Once you have an idea for each type, write a paragraph on it. Compare your choices and paragraphs with those of another student. Discuss your choices.

3. Do the same as in question 2 with an essay that you have written.

4. Do the same as in question 2 with an article in a newspaper or magazine.

HOW ARE YOU GOING TO SAY IT? — CHOOSING YOUR TONE

Now that you've planned your essay and thought about an approach for it, it's time to think about how to say it the best way possible — how to write it as well as you can. To do this, let's start by taking a look at some of the things you do when you speak to people.

Whether you stop to think about it or just do it automatically, you choose a certain way of speaking to a particular person or group of people. Read these bits of conversations and think about how they're different from each other:

EXAMPLE 1

"Hey — what's happening man? Hey, long time no see!"

EXAMPLE 2

"Hello. I'd like to make an appointment to see the doctor about a blood transfusion. If it's at all possible, I'd prefer to book a time in the evening of Friday the 13th, since I'll be free at night."

EXAMPLE 3

"You see, a dominant feature of Canadian writing — one which has tended to subordinate many other aspects of the literature — is 'wilderness.' As I see it, as a metaphor for that which is raw, unexplored, unsettled, the numerous literary depictions of Canada's physical geography serve to reflect a sense of this country in direct relation to the brave and hardy individuals, both indigenous and foreign, who have sought to make this place their home."

Stop for a moment and think about the qualities of each of these examples. For instance, which one would you say is the most casual? Which is the most formal? What about the other one? Where does it fit in?

Well, if you said that the example about "wilderness" in Canadian writing is the most formal sounding of these, you're right. Likewise, if you felt that the example showing two people meeting is the most casual, you're also right. That leaves the example in which someone (something?) is making a doctor's appointment somewhere in between the other two.

The real question here, though, is not just, "Which is the most formal, which is the most casual, and which is in between?" The real question is this: "What did you look at in order to reach your conclusion?"

If you answered that you looked at *the words themselves*, give yourself a pat on the back. It's the words that are being used in each of these bits of conversation that suggest whether the example is expressed formally, casually, or a bit of both. You can judge for yourself simply by testing this out.

🛡️ SPOT CHECK

Look at the words used in example 3. What are they? Pick a few of the most interesting or difficult ones, such as "indigenous," "dominant," "metaphor," "subordinate," "depictions." What do these words mean? Are they words that you're familiar with? If not, check them out in a dictionary. Are you likely to use these words or hear someone else use them during an average day? Is there a particular place you might expect to hear these words?

Now look at some of the other words in this example — "geography," "feature," "writing," "unexplored." Would you be any more likely to use these words or to hear them being used during any day? Are these words more familiar or are they words that you might hear or use in a particular place or situation?

If you thought that most of these words are quite formal or you said to yourself, "I'd probably hear these words being used in college or university," then you've realized something important. You've understood that particular words — and, with them, phrases, figures of speech, and sentence structures — are connected to specific people, places, and situations. Taken together, these words, phrases, figures of speech, and sentence types add up to the *tone* you use — the way you choose to speak to someone.

Just as important, they also amount to the way you choose to *write* to someone. As in speaking to someone, *you're making a choice as to how to say something when you write a letter or an essay.* You can choose to express yourself formally (as in the example you just looked at) or you can choose to express yourself casually (or in any combination).

Similarly, by hearing or reading what you have to say or write, your listener or reader can *detect* your tone by doing what you just did — by examining your words, phrases, and sentences and reaching a conclusion about your tone. Let's try this now for examples 1 and 2.

What are the clues as to the tone being used in example 1? Well, the words themselves are informal sounding, aren't they? Words such as "hey," "man," and short sentences such as "what's happening, man?" and "long time no see" suggest a casual and unexpected meeting between two people. These words and sentences are clearly at the opposite end of the scale from the formal-sounding words and lengthy, complex sentences in example 3.

Now, how would you judge the language and sentences in example 2? Are these formal or informal? The words and sentences in this example are less easy to identify than those in the other examples. For instance, some words and phrases are formal sounding — "appointment," "prefer," "to book a time." But there are at least as many that have a casual sound — contractions such as "I'd," "it's," and "I'll" and words and phrases such as "Hello," "If it's at all possible," and "I'll be free at night." Example 2, then, contains a combination of formal and informal tones.

So where does this analysis of the three examples finally lead? And why should you be concerned about being able to recognize and use different tones when you're speaking or writing?

Well, these three examples show that there are differences in the ways you choose to say something. It's important to see, though, that none of the tones in the examples you've looked at is "correct" in and of itself. In other words, the formal tone of example 3 is neither better than nor preferable to the casual tone of example 1 or the mixed tone of example 2. *The important thing to recognize is that it is the job of the speaker or writer to make sure that the tone is right for a particular listener or reader.*

This is why it's your responsibility as a writer to choose your language for your reader — to think about exactly what your reader means to you when you ask yourself, "How am I going to say this?" You have to think about that person and your relationship to that person when you choose a particular tone. When you take the time to think about which tone you're going to use (which words, phrases, and sentences you're going to pick), you're acknowledging something special about your reader. What you're saying is this: "I respect you and the terms of our relationship enough to communicate with you in the way you expect me to."

By accepting the terms and conditions of that relationship, you show that you want to communicate with people in a tone they expect you to use. For example, if you're writing a résumé and cover letter for a job you want, you'll use the right tone for that situation (if you don't use the expected tone, the chances are good you won't get the job). Similarly, if you're writing to your Aunt Hilda and are aware that there's a good chance that she might invite you to visit her in Europe on your summer vacation (she wants to pay for your flight and all your expenses), you'll write to her in a way that she can understand and be pleased with.

Likewise, as a student writing an essay for your instructor, you need to know the appropriate tone to use for a particular assignment. Even here, the tone you use may vary: a short, informal essay topic may call for an informal, everyday tone, while a long research assignment may require a formal tone. Remember, your choice of tone is neither "right" nor "wrong" — whatever tone you use should be the best choice for that assignment.

So what are the characteristics of a formal or a casual tone for essays? First let's look at what makes up a casual tone.

★ KEY POINTS

Casual Tone

1. *Use everyday words that are easy to understand.* You should use everyday language because the situation calls for it. If you used serious, formal language in a casual situation, it would sound "false," "phony," "put on," or just out of place. The kind of essay that would call for casual words is usually one that asks you to write about some aspect of yourself, a friend or relative, or your personal experiences. In any of these cases, casual language is appropriate because the choice of topic is casual. In reading about such a topic, your reader would likely expect you to use this kind of tone.

2. *Use contractions and colloquialisms.* In a casual writing situation it's all right to use contractions ("I'll" instead of "I will," "don't" instead of "do not") because that's the way people speak in casual circumstances. Similarly, using colloquialisms, or "street talk," is acceptable in a casual essay ("awesome," "bad," "decent," "nerd," "fresh") as long as you show that it's "street talk" by putting quotation marks around it.

3. *Use short sentences.* When we speak casually — to a friend, say — we almost always use short sentences. These short sentences may be complete — "I can't go" — or incomplete —

"Say what?" These sentences are a kind of "shorthand" way of communicating in our everyday speech and have also become acceptable in casual or informal essays.

As you can expect, if these are the characteristics of an informal tone for certain essays, then the opposite characteristics must be the ones used in formal essays.

Formal Tone

1. *The words are complex and often hard to understand.* You wouldn't use complex words just to be difficult or to impress your friends. The real reason you would use them is because such language is a good way to describe abstract, technical, or complex ideas. Because this language creates a "distance" from the reader, it makes it easier to analyze the ideas in a rational way without becoming emotional about them.

2. *Contractions or colloquialisms are not appropriate.* Because the situation is formal, using contractions would not be suitable. The effect of using contractions and colloquialisms in a formal essay would be like wearing blue jeans to a formal dinner party: it's the wrong time and the wrong place. Because the focus in formal writing is on the ideas themselves, casual references would only tend to personalize ideas that are meant to be understood intellectually.

3. *Sentences are long and often balanced with many modifying phrases or clauses.* If you're dealing with abstract or complex ideas, the best way to express their meaning is by using sentences that are themselves complex — again, not just to impress people, but to show the reader the details and subtleties involved in the ideas that you're writing about. Such a sentence might look like this: "Studies show that areas in the spinal cord act as gateways to pain messages that are carried to the brain, where they are amplified, and that, by injecting drugs at these spinal cord sites, the pain messages can be blocked or radically diminished."

A "mixed" type of speaking or writing might be a combination of these formal and casual tones. In example 2, for instance, you saw a mixture of complex words combined with contractions and shorter sentences.

Remember, while teachers often prefer essays to be written in a formal style, don't always assume that to be the case. It's up to you to ask about the suitable tone for each and every assignment.

Finally, if you're more comfortable writing in a casual or mixed tone and your teacher wants you to use a formal one, don't worry. Do your best with the assignment using a dictionary and thesaurus, looking for formal choices for words that you're more familiar with on a casual level.

When you get your essay back, take a good look at what you improved on as well as what you can still improve on. Pay attention to the times you used a word or a sentence well. At the same time, look at the comments that show how you might have done something better. If you can't understand the comments on your essay or if your teacher didn't write any, make an appointment to have your work explained to you. Don't just throw your essay away or into a corner without looking at it first. Each time you write something and get it back with comments on it, you've got an opportunity to learn something about what you did this time, and what you can do the next time. Take it. Use it.

☼ HIGHLIGHTS

- It's you, the writer, who chooses the tone.
- You choose the tone with your reader and his or her expectations in mind.
- You choose an appropriate tone because you respect the relationship you have with your reader.
- Using a particular tone for an essay is not an accident; it's part of your deliberate decision to express yourself to someone in a particular way.
- If you have difficulty finding the right tone for a writing assignment, think of the tone you would use when speaking to your reader about a topic.
- It's your job to find out from your instructor which tone is right for a particular essay.
- You can change your tone if you find that it's not the best choice for that essay.

✍ **THINGS TO DO**

1. You meet a friend at a record store and get into a conversation. Think of something that you might say. First, talk to yourself. Say what you would actually say to this person. Once you've done that, write down your response. Compare it with another student's response. What tone are you using? How can you tell?

2. You have a meeting with a counsellor at an employment centre. You describe your experience, education, and the type of job you're looking for. What tone are you using here? Point out some characteristics of your tone.

3. You're driving along and a police car pulls you over. A police officer approaches your car. What would you likely say? Why? Identify your tone and its characteristics.

4. Look at these writing samples and say something about the tone of each one:

   a) Italian casual-wear maker Benetton unveiled its latest advertising campaign recently, one likely to be as controversial as some of its predecessors. One of the new print ads features models dressed like a priest and a nun kissing on the lips. Another ad shows a newborn baby still bloody from birth and with its umbilical cord unsevered. "The images aren't aimed at showing off the beauty of the clothing but at capturing the interest of people with the aim of making them reflect," said Oliviero Toscani, the photographer who created the ads.

   b) Sexism is supposed to be dead in the egalitarian Nordic countries, but it still haunts the home and corporate boardrooms. The socialist democracies of northern Europe take pride in 20 years of tough laws against sex discrimination. Norway, Sweden, Denmark, Finland, and Iceland rank high in surveys on the status of women. Citizens publicly embrace equality and women challenge men for political leadership. Despite these gains, however, women still trail men in pay and opportunity.

c) The latest in food rages in Japan is to eat fish live — flounder that flap on the plate, finger-length eel swallowed raw. And remember, if the shrimp don't dance, send 'em back. "The food moves around a lot; that's the whole idea," says the chef at a well-known restaurant. Waiters bring the fish in wiggling, their eyes and mouths moving, then quickly slice open the mid-section and gut it, so the fish is ready to eat. Like sushi or sashimi, the slices are dipped in a mixture of soy sauce and horseradish.

5. Bring a magazine to class and look for an article that interests you. Work with another student and analyze its tone.

6. Look at an essay you're working on. What can you say about the tone you're using in it?

THINK ABOUT YOUR READER — WHO ARE YOU WRITING THIS FOR ANYWAY?

You never do anything in a vacuum. In other words, everything you do affects someone else. If you stay out late, your parents get worried. If you don't pay the rent, your landlord gets angry. If you send someone flowers, you make that person happy. Whatever you do, someone else is affected.

It's the same with writing. Whatever you write affects someone else. If you write a letter to your girlfriend saying that you miss her and can't wait to see her during Christmas break or the summer holidays, you're certainly affecting someone else.

As you just saw in the previous section, *how* you say something is definitely a part of your relationship with another person. Well, it's the same situation when you think about *what* you say to your reader. If you want to affect your reader in the best way possible, you need to think about who that person is and what to say to that person.

Every time you write an essay, you're asking yourself this question: "How is what I'm writing going to affect the person who reads this?" And every time you ask this question you're really thinking about your reader; you're thinking of who your reader is and what that person needs to know. At various points in this chapter, you've already stopped and thought about the person you're writing for. When you asked yourself, "How does this person relate to my topic?" or "What is the best way I can say this to that person?" you were thinking of your reader.

Well, now is a good time to do it again. When your research has led you to your answer and you've chosen your best points to back it up, stop and ask yourself these questions:

- "Who am I writing this for?"
- "What does this person know about my topic?"
- "What does this person need to know about my topic?"

Let's look at how this works.

When you buy a gift for a friend, you have to ask yourself certain questions before you make that purchase: "Does he have one of these already?", "Does he need one?", "Would he even like one?" This is the kind of questioning you do on an everyday basis about things that affect yourself and other people.

You do a similar kind of questioning when you write something. When you're writing a card or a letter to a friend or relative, the things that you choose to write about (as well as those you omit) are done with your reader in mind.

Most of the time you're not really even aware that you're doing this. For example, if you're filling out an application for student financial aid, you're selecting your points automatically. You're writing your application and aiming your answers at questions like these: "How much money will you need?", "How much can you contribute from your savings and summer job?", "How much can your parents contribute?"

What you won't write about in your application is "How I enjoyed my summer" or "Why my parents want me to go to college." You won't write about these things because the application *doesn't need to know* about them. They may be interesting things to know and may even be somewhat related to what you are being asked to write about, but *they're not part of the specific answer itself*, and you wouldn't include them. Even in an application you're paying attention to what your reader needs to know.

And it's the same with the other cases you've looked at. For instance, in his explanation to Tina, Tom gives her only those points that are relevant to his answer, only those points that she needs to know to answer her question about the popularity of The Rolling Stones. Although he probably discovered other information in his "research" (Mick Jagger's age, Charlie Watts's favourite colour), he realizes it doesn't belong, so he doesn't make it part of his answer or essay.

The same happens in Lisa Leegull's defence of Kristy Kleer. Lisa probably found out much about Kristy and her life that she wouldn't bother telling the jury. The only things she does include in her "essay" to the jury are those things she thinks are absolutely necessary to convince them of Kristy's innocence. She makes a clear decision about who her "readers" are and what they need to know. Behind the evidence she ultimately presents to the jury is the "unseen activity" of selecting her points with them in mind; by presenting the jury with the things she does (and by omitting all those that don't help her case), Lisa shows that she's made careful choices about what the jury needs to know and what it doesn't. In short, to come up with the best answer possible, she's thinking of her "readers."

You also see this process happening in the example of car safety. If you're writing an essay about this topic for an auto mechanics course, you might choose the points that deal with the mechanical features of car safety: brake lights, brakes, and seatbelts. In this case, you know your instructor will be more concerned about these features than other ones. However, if the essay is for an instructor who teaches a course in driver training or insurance, you'll probably choose the other points to make your case: driver training, insurance, and road emergency club membership. Here, too, you're paying special attention to who your reader is and what your reader needs to know.

All of these are examples of "thinking about your reader." In each case, no one is writing anything in a vacuum. Instead, the writers are making a thoughtful assessment of who the readers are, of what they already know, and of what they need to know. This kind of thinking shows that you're paying special attention to the person you're writing your essay for; and that that attention will help you decide what to leave in and what to leave out.

Remember, not all people need or want to know the same information. So by thinking about your readers, you're making your job easier for yourself and for them.

☼ HIGHLIGHTS

- In coming up with your topic or in answering it, you take your readers and what they need to know into account.

- Thinking about your reader helps you focus your answer; if you know what this person needs to know, you'll know exactly what to put into your answer.

✍ THINGS TO DO

1. Think about going to an interview for a job you'd like. Write down some of the things you think the interviewer would need to know about you. Which of these points are the most important ones?

Which are the least important? Narrow your list down to three or four points, and compare your results with those of a classmate.

2. Imagine that you're getting married and that your future mother-in-law is interviewing you to find out why you think you're the best choice for her daughter or son. What would she need to know about you to convince her? Compare your list with someone else's.

3. Look at an article in a newspaper or magazine. What is it saying? What do you think it might have left out? What kind of reader is it aimed at? How can you tell? Discuss your answers in class.

4. Do the same as in question 3 with an essay you have written.

CHAPTER 4

BUILDING YOUR ESSAY

WORKING OUT THE MAIN POINTS IN A PARAGRAPH

What exactly do you do when you write something? Well, as you've already seen, when you write something, you're actually *putting what you think down on paper*. Your writing doesn't come from any "mysterious" or "magical" source; what you *think* about a certain subject is what you *write* about it.

But if you actually write what you think, what kind of form or structure will you end up with? In other words, is there any orderly shape that you can give to your thoughts?

Well, for most of what you think during any given day, the answer to this is really *no*. The thoughts that occur to you daily are mostly random and fleeting. They don't occur in any particular order, and they don't often stay in your mind for too long.

But this is only natural. When the situation does not demand it, you don't pay special attention to any particular thoughts. For example, when you're driving, you (hopefully) give some of your attention to the road and to other drivers, but you also think of other things as well — an upcoming party, a dentist's appointment, the grocery shopping, and your favourite tune on the radio are just some examples.

You may give equal time to each of these things, or you may give more time to one than to another. You may intermingle your thoughts about all of them, or you may not think about them in any conscious order. That's just the way it is when you think about things in a casual way, when your thinking is "hanging loose."

However, when the situation demands it, you're capable of thinking in another way: in an ordered or structured way. When your rent cheque "bounces," when your car is towed away, or when your best friend has an accident and is taken to the hospital, you're quite able to focus your thinking on the matter at hand and keep it there for as long as you need to. And it's just as easy for you to do this when the events are happy ones: when your student loan comes through, when you get the summer job you wanted, when you plan a mid-term vacation.

At moments like these, when the situation calls for it, you're ready and able to think long and hard about what you need to. You think about what has happened, what is happening, what might happen, what has been done about it, and what you can do about it. In demanding situations, you're able to marshal your thoughts on a subject or situation.

Even later, when someone asks, "What were you thinking at that particular time?" you're able to recall and retell your thoughts in a fairly accurate way. In fact, when you're remembering something, you discover that you're arranging your "story" in the best way possible. That's not to say that you're changing it or lying about it. It's just that in reflecting upon it, you take the opportunity to give it the shape or structure that makes it clear and understandable for both yourself and your listener.

When you do this, you give your thoughts *form* — you present them in segments to make it easy for your listener to understand and follow them. For example: "Well, let me tell you, the first frightening thing I thought of was.... *Then* I tried to call.... After a while, I had to give up and hope that.... When I finally got there.... Wow! Did I feel better when I saw that...." These are the "pieces" of your story and the thoughts that you've made into "chunks" of information so that the person who's listening to you can understand your story.

And you'd do the same thing if you were to write about it. You'd want to give shape, structure, or form to your thoughts so that your reader could easily understand them and follow you.

This, then, is where *paragraphs* come in. When you write in paragraphs, all you're really doing is using the paragraph to give shape or structure to your thoughts. This means that every paragraph has these two parts to it: *structure* (the shape or "look" of the paragraph itself) and *content* (the thinking that goes on in it). Let's see how this works.

🚌 SPOT CHECK

Let's look at *content* first. Each main idea you have about a topic should be worked out in *one* paragraph. What you're doing is putting a reasonable framework on your thinking. If you were to put two or three or more ideas into one paragraph, it wouldn't take long to see that you couldn't tell one idea from the other — they'd all be jumbled together. For example, if you write about what kind of job you looked for today, how you went about looking for it, how you applied for it, and what the results were, you'd want to keep each one of these ideas separate from the others by writing about it in its own paragraph. What this means, then, is that if you have three main ideas, you'll have three paragraphs; if you have ten ideas, you'll have ten paragraphs; and so on. So, when you use one paragraph to "contain" each idea, the people you're writing to will easily be able to tell by the content where one idea begins and where it ends.

They can also tell, though, by looking at the *structure* of the paragraph. Everybody knows what a paragraph looks like: that it begins with an indentation, that it is made up of a number of sentences, and that it ends with a blank space. In fact, whether it's long or short, every paragraph looks something like this:

_____
_____
_____
_____
_____
_____
_____
_____
_____
_____.

What the structure of every paragraph really does is send you a series of "signals" about what you're reading or writing. The indentation at the beginning tells you that the idea is beginning; the sentences tell you what the idea is and something about it; and the blank space at the end says that this idea is finished and that you should get ready to move on to another one. These points about structure and content may seem fairly basic and straightforward, but they're important for two reasons.

One reason is that they're helpful guides to understanding paragraphs for both readers and writers. The structure of a paragraph is a clear indicator to both the reader and the writer of where an idea starts and where it stops. As an "external" indicator, the structure of a paragraph helps the writer, who has to know where to begin and end an idea, and the reader, who is trying to understand the idea. As well, as an "internal" indicator, content is equally important. Knowing that each paragraph contains the development of only one idea, the reader can know what to expect, and the writer has a guide to "weed out" what shouldn't be in a paragraph and to add what could be missing.

The second reason has to do with understanding the connection between paragraph structure and content. While you need a structure to "show" each idea, it's important to remember that the structure doesn't dictate how you develop an idea. Look at it this way. A paragraph has a kind of set, or "fixed," shape; except for length, one paragraph looks much like any other. In terms of how it looks, then, a paragraph acts as a structure or "container" that allows an idea to be developed within its "space."

Writing in paragraphs also has a lot to do with the idea of an essay as an answer. If an essay is an answer, then a paragraph must be *part* of the answer or the development of *one main point* in that answer. Because you have a number of main points — each related to the other, but each different from the other — you need a "device" to show their connectedness. That's why you use paragraphs.

★ KEY POINTS

1. When you write an essay as an answer, you make a conscious decision to show someone your thinking on a topic. Because you want your reader to follow your thoughts, it only makes sense to use paragraphs as signposts, or signals, to make the job as easy as possible.

2. Writing reflects your thinking: What you think about is what you write about. So, if writing something down is like taking a snapshot of your thinking, then focusing an idea in a paragraph is like taking a snapshot of that idea. If you want your reader to agree with your answer, then you have to "freeze-frame" your thoughts so that someone else can read them and understand them. The best way to do this is to use clear, well-defined paragraphs to "pin down" your ideas.

3. When you're simply moving from one thought to another during any ordinary day, you don't have to express your ideas in a developed or coherent way. However, when you write an essay you must think and write in a certain way, to make your answer as clear as possible for yourself and your reader. As the examples at the beginning of this section show, when you need to do so you are able to focus your response to a situation that calls for it. And that's all you're really doing here. By using paragraphs to "hold" your ideas, you're presenting the main points of an answer in a way that makes it easy for your reader to understand them.

4. In general, there's no "ideal" length for a paragraph. Ideas come in all shapes and sizes, and so do the paragraphs that present those ideas. When you write a paragraph you try to do justice to the particular idea it develops, and that means making the paragraph the "right" size for each idea. Remember, if your thinking about your topic determines the length of your essay, then the same is true of a paragraph: the amount of thinking you do on any particular idea is what determines the length of any paragraph.

5. A paragraph is really like a "mini-essay." Just as an essay is a clear and specific answer to an essay topic, *a paragraph is a clear and specific part of that answer*. And just as you ask, "What is this essay trying to prove?" so should you ask about each paragraph, "What is this paragraph trying to prove?" In this way, if you know what each paragraph is about, then you'll include only what is relevant to that paragraph and leave out everything that doesn't belong.

6. Like an essay, a paragraph has the same three parts: *an introduction, a body, and a conclusion*. Your conclusion is the last sentence, and it should state strongly what point that paragraph is making; the sentences you write to support your idea in the paragraph make up the body; and the first sentence of the paragraph is an introduction that announces the topic or the idea of that paragraph. Using this structure is relatively easy; you're not doing anything new or different from what

you've already done in thinking out your essay. All you're doing is repeating the same pattern to make clear each of the points you're using to support your answer.

7. Don't forget that, as with an essay, *you can change any paragraph* if you don't like it or if it can be replaced with a better one. As you learned in "Planning Your Answer" in Chapter 3, if you decide to change any of the main points that you use to support your answer, you can easily change the paragraph that you're using to develop it. You're not locked into anything.

☼ HIGHLIGHTS

- A paragraph is a "snapshot" of your answer. If your essay says that "the World Wrestling Federation bouts on television are phony because of these reasons," each of your reasons is part of your answer and you'd use a paragraph to give a picture of each of those reasons.

- Paragraphs are signals; they tell you and your reader where an idea begins and where it ends.

- Writing in paragraphs shows that you're using a pattern or structure to give an answer.

✍ THINGS TO DO

1. Here are some paragraphs from students' essays on various topics. After you've read each one, answer these questions about it:

   a) Does the last sentence give a conclusion?

   b) Does the body give facts or examples to back up the conclusion?

   c) Does the first sentence suggest what the paragraph is about?

d) Is the paragraph complete? Is it developed enough, or are there other things that could have been added?

e) Are there things that could have been left out?

f) What would you do to improve it overall?

Rewrite each paragraph to your satisfaction.

Compare your responses with those of another student.

Paragraph 1

One ingredient of a successful relationship is understanding. Without understanding, the most common emotion that occurs is resentment. If one partner wants to go out dancing while the other wants to stay at home because he or she is not feeling well, there should be some understanding from the partner who wants to go out. That person has to realize that he or she can't always do what he or she wants because there is another person involved. At the same time, if the one person still wanted to go out dancing, then understanding has to be shown by the sick partner. He or she should realize that, just because one person is sick, that's no reason for the other one not to be able to go out.

Paragraph 2

Unfortunately, many people who buy lottery tickets live for the weekly draw. They take all the extra money they can find and will buy a ridiculous number of tickets, hoping to increase their chances. Some believe that it's just a matter of time before their numbers are drawn. These attitudes are certainly not healthy. Believing they are about to become millionaires at any moment, some tend to rely on this windfall before they have it. Spending all their money on lottery tickets is a good example of this. They believe it's worth it since they're going to get it all back in due time. Some may even spend beyond their means while indulging in their fantasy of wealth.

Paragraph 3

You must also be mature to have children. If you have six, you must be able to love all six equally and be impartial with them. Some people have a marked preference for their first born or for the youngest one. Some men love their sons more than they do their daughters because they are copies of their former youthful selves. Although these feelings are all human, they are quite hurtful. How many times have you heard the middle child complain that it is neither the cherished eldest nor the pampered baby? If you make the decision to have children, you should be prepared to be impartial. It is hard to hide certain preferences for a special child, but what you have to do is distribute your attention and love equally.

Paragraph 4

Communication is a key component in establishing a successful relationship. Although it may be difficult to create proper channels of communication, somehow these difficulties must be overcome. Right from the beginning, a couple should be frank and open with each other so they can fully understand what they really like. Maintaining good communication is also vital. Always touching upon new areas of interest and creating lively conversations are ways of maintaining communication. If the two people can communicate well with each other, then their relationship has a good chance of becoming a success.

Paragraph 5

As well as the problems that arise from unrealistic expectations, there are also problems that result when someone actually wins a lottery. With the huge amounts of money being given away these days, a winner could receive millions and millions of dollars. When people find themselves in a situation of excess wealth, their judgement can become impaired. For example, many families have ended up in court fighting over who gets what percentage of the winnings. Others might actually desert their families in order to enjoy the money themselves. Many winners try to go on living normal lives, but find it is nearly impossible. As soon as their names are publicly announced, they are hounded by every charitable (and non-charitable) organization known to mankind. This cannot be a pleasant experience. Changes must be made to the lotteries to prevent the disruption and even corruption of people's lives.

✍ THINGS TO DO

2. Do the same things in question 1 with the paragraphs in an essay you recently wrote.

3. Do the same things in question 1 with the paragraphs in a magazine article.

ARRANGING YOUR PARAGRAPHS

Not only do paragraphs have to make sense, but the order in which you put them has to, too. You could write brilliant paragraphs that sparkle and shine individually like diamonds. But, by putting them together to create an overall pattern, you can create a much more dazzling effect.

When you come up with the right points to support your answer, what you do with each one is a major factor in presenting your reader with the best evidence for your answer. You saw this with both Tom and Lisa Leegull. They chose their best points carefully so that they would be believed. But you also saw that they had to do something with those points, that they had to put them in the best order. Not doing so would have left the points scattered all over the place. Like diamonds, the reader could still have appreciated each one by itself, but not nearly as much as when they are joined together in a "bracelet" or "necklace."

The essays and examples throughout this book arrange their paragraphs in different ways. Let's look at some of these ways, or *orders*, to see how they can help you sort your main points.

⭐ KEY POINTS

1. *Logical order.* As the word suggests, a logical order is one that "makes sense": there should be a sensible relation between the

points. In addition, each point has to make sense before a following point can be understood. Let's say that you're describing how someone you know has become a street kid. You would relate the causes and the effects in the order in which they make sense: "Yeah, he had a really rough time at home, and he didn't do well at school. He also started hanging around with the wrong kinds of kids and getting into trouble. Now he's living on the street and he hasn't got anyone to turn to for help." This is a logical relation of points because your reader has to know what happened first in order to fully understand what came later.

2. *Chronological order.* In some cases, this type of order might make the most sense for your paragraphs because it lets you connect them in order of time. If you relate your paragraphs in terms of first, second, third, and so on, because they happened one after the other, then you're using chronological order. Let's say that someone asks you, "What did you do from the time you got up today till now?" Chances are you'll go through whatever highlights you think are worth giving from the time they happened until this moment in the order in which they occurred: "Well, after I got up this morning, I got ready for work.... Then I headed for the bus stop.... When I got to work I started to.... Then I had lunch with my best friend.... The afternoon dragged by until.... Now I'm talking to you...." If there's a natural "time relationship" between your main points, you'd do well to put them in chronological order.

3. *Order of growing importance.* In this case, you think about and "weigh" your main points to see which is more important than another. You have to look at each one, understand how it relates to the other points, and then put them in order from strong to stronger to strongest. You've seen this kind of connecting before when Tom weighed his points about The Rolling Stones and when Lisa considered the order in which she chose to present the points of her evidence. You will probably use this method of arranging your points for most of your essays. By ordering your points this way, you're saying to your reader: "These are the reasons I believe this. Now I'm going to give them

to you starting with the good ones and ending with the *great* ones."

4. *Random order.* The word "random" means "haphazard" or "having no order." If you find that your paragraphs can't be connected in any of the ways you've just looked at, then you could put them in random order. What you're saying here is that each paragraph is equal to the others in importance and, there being no real connection between any of them, you're free to present them in any order you choose.

What's important to remember is that the order you choose for your paragraphs isn't something that you "take" from somewhere and impose on your points. Rather, the order already exists among the paragraphs themselves. When you see an answer in a certain way, you must already see the main points behind that answer in a certain way (remember, they led you to your answer).

The more you think about them, the main points behind any answer usually have a way of sorting themselves out and connecting themselves. One day you may see one point as having great importance, the next day it's out, replaced by another; one day this order makes the most sense, another day it's the worst possible choice. None of these shifts should cause you any concern. All you're doing is reassessing your thinking and, with it, the relationships between your "big" ideas. Go with the flow.

☼ HIGHLIGHTS

- While each of your paragraphs is important for what it says, together they say much more.

- There are different ways to make sense of the relationship between your paragraphs.

- Order isn't something that you impose externally on your paragraphs; rather, it's the relationship that exists between them already and that is strongly suggested by the content of the paragraphs themselves.

✍ THINGS TO DO

1. Here is a student essay in which the paragraphs (including the introduction and conclusion) are mixed up (each paragraph itself is intact, though). Arrange the paragraphs so that they're in the order in which they were intended to be. When you've done that, tell how you recognize what order to use; where did you get your idea? Now that you have them in the "right" order, identify which order it is. How do you know? Why? How many of the kinds of orders you've looked at could you put these points in? Will all of them work? Why or why not?

Boys and Girls, Girls and Boys

Young boys of today are watching as girls the same age are being encouraged to become what they want to be. In today's society, it is possible for a woman to enter predominantly male professions such as engineering and police work. Young boys accept this as normal and are also encouraged to become nurses and secretaries. Both of these careers have long been viewed as women's jobs. In today's society, men are not considered to be "less of a man" to be involved in such professions.

Little boys are growing up in a more equal society in which women are seen to be more than the '50s stereotype of "barefoot, pregnant and in the kitchen." Young boys' views overall have changed to accept today's independent women, a fact that is making society better for all of us.

Boys of today's generation are growing up in a society in which women are taking a more active role in that society. Either out of necessity or for pleasure, women today are working in businesses and corporations and earning nearly as much as men in the same positions. Young boys are seeing their mothers work as hard or, in some circumstances, harder than their fathers to bring home a pay cheque. Boys today are taking this as the normal way of life, and they don't have the same preconceived ideas of what a woman should or should not do.

Little boys of today are less chauvinistic than their fathers were as boys. The ideals and views of young boys today are vastly different from those of young boys of the '50s. Young boys of today are growing up in a society where they are encouraged to participate with young girls in various sorts of activities, where women are employed in careers that were once only men's jobs, and where women are taking a more active role in the business world and society.

In today's society, boys and girls are involved together in more activities than they were in the past, either in sports or academics. Typically in the past, boys and girls were involved in separate activities, which enforced the idea that girls weren't strong enough to compete against boys. In today's society, girls and boys work and play alongside each other, and this encourages boys to treat girls as their equals.

✍ THINGS TO DO

2. Write two or three paragraphs using each of the types of orders described in this section.

3. Look at the essays in this book and identify the order in which the paragraphs are arranged. Would any other order make sense? Why or why not?

4. Do the same as in question 3 with an essay of yours.

5. Do the same as in question 3 with an article from a newspaper or magazine.

MOVING FROM ONE PARAGRAPH TO ANOTHER

Just as street signs help you make sense of where you are and where you're going, certain words or phrases show your reader the direction your thinking takes.

If a friend of yours is a first-time visitor to your city, you'd want to show him the local sights — a clothing store, a record store, a bar, a park, and a dance club. You'd also show him how to get from one place to another in a way that makes sense. After a while, your friend would have a fairly good idea of the "big picture" — the whole city itself.

It's the same with writing. Your paragraphs are like the specific locations you take your reader to; they're the developed ideas you want your reader to understand. At the same time, though, you want to show how you got from one point to the other so that your reader, like your visitor, understands the connections between the ideas as well as you do. Ultimately, the clearer you make the signposts between the ideas, the more likely your readers will understand the "big picture" — the whole essay.

Let's look at an example of how to use words and phrases to connect ideas. Say that you're showing someone your photo album. You've done a lot of work putting it into chronological order, starting with your very earliest pictures and moving to the latest. As you're describing your photos, you tell the story behind each one (as you would in a paragraph): "That's one of me when I was five years old and the melted chocolate bar in my hand ended up in Santa's beard." But, besides "telling the story" about each photo, you'd also give your friend an idea of *how they're connected* by saying things like, "This is a picture of me when I was two and had the longest, curliest hair, *and this next one* is one of me just six months later when my hair was almost shaved off!" These "connectors," "transitions," or "time markers" help your friend make sense of how the photos are related to each other; having heard the connections between all the pictures, this person would then have a very strong sense of how the whole album fits together.

Just as your paragraphs are snapshots of your ideas, the words and phrases you use to connect them help your reader to understand how they're related, how you got from one to the other, and, finally, how they all fit together to show your answer in the best way possible. What are these connectors? Well, they're words or phrases such as these:

and	for instance	obviously
also	furthermore	of course
although	generally	on the other hand
as well	however	specifically
because	in addition	still
but	in fact	therefore
certainly	in other words	thus
consequently	in short	to conclude
finally	indeed	undoubtedly
first, second, third,	moreover	usually
for example	nevertheless	yet

How should you use these connectors? For starters, look at the last section on arranging your paragraphs. There you saw that it's necessary to look at the paragraphs (the ideas) themselves to see how they are connected in your answer. Once you know what the connection is, then choose from these words and phrases to express it.

Remember, the transitions are there to express the relationship between your ideas. If those relationships are clear in your mind, then you'll be able to provide the necessary link between them. If those relationships change, find another link.

☼ HIGHLIGHTS

- Transitions, or links, are words and phrases that show the relationship between your ideas.

- If you change your ideas, then find different links to show the changed connections between them.

✏️ THINGS TO DO

Discuss the following activities in class:

1. Sort out the essay at the end of the previous section, "Arranging Your Paragraphs," and figure out the connections between the paragraphs. Then put in transitions that show those connections.

2. Examine the transitions in the other essays in this book. Do they make sense? Are there others that could be used?

3. Pick a section in this book and do the same as in question 2. Explain the choices that have been made.

4. Take an essay of yours and do the same as in question 2.

5. Take a magazine or newspaper article and do the same as in question 2.

THE LONGER ESSAY

So far, the essay examples that you've looked at have been relatively short ones—200 to 300 words or one to two pages long. It's now time to take a big step and look at a longer essay.

Recall that at the end of the section called "Four Advantages of the Common Sense Approach" in Chapter 2, you saw that one of the advantages is knowing that *an essay is flexible*; that is, as long as you're clear about what your answer is, your essay can be either a short, medium, or long response. It can be whatever length you need it to be or want it to be.

The important thing about this point is that the difference in the length of any essay isn't something that's just a "fluke," or "luck," or "artificial." Instead, the difference in essay length is determined only *by the amount of thinking* and, therefore, *the amount of writing* that you do about any given essay topic.

The more ideas you come up with to develop your answer, the longer your essay will be. Similarly, the more facts, evidence, and proof you come up with, the longer your essay becomes. There's no "magical" or "mysterious" reason as to why one essay is longer than another; it's just that one student has thought about and researched an answer more than another student has.

Let's take a look at a longer essay to see how it's both different from and yet similar to the shorter ones you've looked at up to now. The following essay was written by a student named Jasmine; it can be called a "long" essay because Jasmine's writing (without the footnote or bibliography pages) totalled a little over five typed, double-spaced pages (approximately 1400 words) when it was finished. The essay is called "Body Image" and was written for a college course in Mass Media and Culture. Read the essay carefully with these questions in mind:

1. Does the conclusion say clearly and strongly what the essay is trying to prove?
2. Does the introduction state what the essay is trying to prove?
3. What points do the paragraphs talk about?
4. Are the paragraphs arranged in any kind of order?
5. Are the paragraphs connected to each other?
6. What can you say about the tone?

Body Image

P1 All too often, a woman's sense of her body is created by her culture, causing her to see herself and others in a certain way. In our case, Western culture tells women that they can "never be too thin." If women do not measure up to this ideal of weight and body shape, it looks as though they have no self-control and they are feared, hated, and isolated. The mass media in our culture creates an ideal body image. Even though most women cannot live up to this image, all women are made to feel that they must try to in order to be seen as "complete." This type of media and social control causes women to judge themselves and each other by how acceptable their body image is in their society.

P2 The media's idea of the "perfect" female form has a tremendous persuasive influence on women. As they grow up, women are pressured by society to look and behave in certain ways. They learn to think of themselves mainly in terms of how they appear externally. Early in a woman's life, she is given the message that she must look "good" in order to become an accepted member of society and to please men. From a very young age, girls believe the myth that to be attractive and successful people they must be thin and remain thin at all costs.

P3 Adolescent girls in particular are taught to see the ideal woman as having a perfect body (Ussher, 39). Media messages play a large role in warning young women to be afraid of their bodies if they are not "perfect" because imperfections will result in "abnormal" social interactions. For example, gaining weight when a young girl goes through puberty is a natural process of the female body, but through the media these girls are told that a thin body brings happiness, popularity and helps her to entice a man, which she is further told is her main objective. This attitude, set in adolescence, continues throughout a woman's life, resulting in dissatisfaction with her body and constant worry over her appearance and weight.

P4 Increasingly, women in North America are bombarded with images of the ideal woman. At no time in the past has there ever been such intense media coverage telling women what they should look like. The idea that women should be thin is placed in our minds everywhere we go by strategic media gimmicks and advertisements (Boston, 5). All women are judged by others and judge themselves against the image of the ideal woman. Without exception, this image is that of a tall, shapely, young, glamorous, white, heterosexual woman. She may change from decade to decade depending on the current fashions—big breasts or small ones, a full figure or a slim one—but, no matter what the popular image is at any time, women are always pressured into copying it, even if it means drastically changing their natural appearance with cosmetics or plastic surgery. Today, for example, many women are enlarging their breasts and their lips because the media tells them that cleavage and a full mouth are in style. The media displays these messages and images on television and movie screens, on billboards and in fashion magazines (Boston, 6). However, these messages and images too often leave out all the women who are not white or Anglo-Saxon and who end up feeling torn between North America's cultural standards and the standards of their own culture (Boston, 6).

P5 The single aim of hundreds of profit-making corporations is to convince women that they do not look good enough or do not meet the standard body image. Whole industries depend on selling women products through slick ads that show only the standardized, beautiful woman (Boston, 6). These advertisements work on women's insecurities about their bodies and their fears of imperfection. Most women have a natural desire to want to look and feel good; they want to wear colours and materials that make them feel attractive, appreciated, and beautiful. The problem begins when the media defines "beautiful" in very narrow terms, making women feel that they will never achieve true beauty. For example, if a woman is different from the standard form, if she is fat or physically disabled, she has to deal with extreme forms of societal pressure and ridicule, openly and daily. Women who do not fit the ideal image experience the pain of negative judgements, fears, and hatreds in subtle or unsubtle ways. This negative attitude toward women who do not fit the model makes it difficult for them to love and accept themselves as they are.

P6 The majority of women in our culture do not accept their bodies as they are. In fact, it is rare to find a woman with a healthy body image who is not actively doing battle with her body (Hutchinson, 26). Almost every woman is unhappy about all or some parts of her body. Her hair is too straight or too curly, her nose is too large or too small, her breasts are too big or too small, her stomach or thighs are too fat, her frame is too bony, or she is too short. Because of a negative body image, many women try to hide their bodies from view and feel ashamed of their bodies, even with friends or lovers. Consequently, they struggle to imitate the standard image of beauty. They do this by shaving their body hair, applying make-up, exercising, and dieting. And still women often compare themselves to others and are convinced that they could never be happy or even satisfied the way they are. Even if other people say they are beautiful, they do not or cannot believe them because the media dictates that they can never be too beautiful.

P7 Approximately 90 percent of women in Canada have some degree of body dissatisfaction (Sheinin, 1). Advertisements for diets, for example, are usually aimed at women, and articles on dieting and exercising are common in women's magazines (Sheinin, 2). Consequently, the effects of this preoccupation to fit the image often range from occasional dieting to serious eating disorders, extreme depression, and dangerous weight-loss surgery (Hutchinson, 26). Statistics show that 90 to 95 percent of people with eating disorders are women. Anorexia nervosa, bulimia, and obesity are reaching epidemic proportions. Similarly, over 80 percent of women have dieted by the age of eighteen, and 40 percent of nine-year-olds have already started their first diet. Even at the ages of three, four, and five, there has been an expressed wish to diet (Sheinin, 2). Studies show that dieting is usually not successful in the long run and that repeated low-calorie dieting is even a major cause of ill health. These problems are all responses to the enormous pressures on women to be thin.

P8 The average North American fashion model is five feet (152 cm), eight inches (20 cm) tall and weighs 115 pounds (52.27 kg); the average North American woman is five feet (152 cm), three inches (7.6 cm) tall and weighs 144 pounds (65.45 kg). The model weighs 20 percent less than the average woman (Sheinin, 3). This contrast is a perfect example of how the media does not give the public reasonable images to strive for. With a body that does not fit the standard media image, women learn very quickly what society expects from them. The message given to women by the fashion and diet industries is that they are never good enough, that they must constantly deprive themselves and continually fight the natural size of their bodies. The promotion of a beauty ideal is practically an impossible achievement for the majority of women.

P9 There is an important question that women must ask themselves. Why must they diet and continually deprive themselves in order to achieve a "beautiful" body and be accepted by North American standards? The impossible beauty ideal that is created by society through the media is precisely that: impossible. This impossible ideal gives society a reason to hate and fear the female form because of the lack of control women have over the shape of their natural physique. Society's lack of respect for and even hatred of a woman's natural body have established extremely narrow guidelines for what is seen as attractive, sexy, and powerful. Women of all shapes, sizes, ages, physical abilities, races, and classes should be able to feel good about themselves and their natural forms. They should refuse to follow the guidelines set by the media by taking back their body images and reclaiming them as their own. Women should be able to celebrate their female forms, no matter what size, shape, or colour that form may take.

Works Cited

Boston Women's Health Book Collective. The New Our Bodies, Ourselves. New York: Simon & Shuster Inc., 1984.

Brown, Laura S. and Esther D. Rothenblum, eds. Fat Oppression and Psychotherapy: A Feminist Perspective. New York: The Haworth Press, 1989.

Gillman, Sander L. Sexuality: An Illustrated History. New York: John Wiley & Son, 1989.

Hutchinson, Marcia Germaine. Transforming Body Image: Learning to Love the Body You Have. Washington: Library of Congress, 1985.

Sheinin, Rachel. "Body Shame: Body Image in a Cultural Context." Bulletin 5, no.5. Toronto: National Eating Disorder Information Centre, 1990.

Ussher, Jane M. The Psychology of the Female Body. London: Routledge, 1989.

All right, now that you've read Jasmine's longer essay, what can you say about it? How is this essay both different from and similar to the other essays you've looked at? Probably the best starting point is to say some specific things about the questions just before the essay. Let's do that now.

SPOT CHECK

1. *Does the conclusion state clearly and strongly what the essay is trying to prove?* Well, it looks as though all of the sentences in the last paragraph emphasize some aspect of the answer: that society, particularly through the media, encourages women to judge themselves according to an artificial ideal of beauty. For instance, the question at the beginning of the conclusion addresses the issue of why things are the way they are; it asks, "Why do women deprive themselves in order to fit in with someone else's idea of beauty?" The next sentence gives a natural and reasonable response to this question by saying that society's idea of perfect beauty is impossible to achieve and maintain. The next two sentences carry this logical build-up to the heart of the issue. They look at the results of women's dissatisfaction when they don't measure up to society's image of beauty: society and the media hate and fear the natural female form because it's the result (they think) of women's lack of self-control over their bodies; therefore, both society and the

media end up setting narrow guidelines for what they consider beautiful. Finally, the last three sentences propose a solution by saying that all women should reject the artificial guidelines for beauty and should, instead, rejoice in their natural form, whatever that form may be. When you check what all of these sentences say against what the answer is, you can see that this conclusion is a powerful statement of what this essay is trying to prove.

2. *Does the introduction state what the essay is trying to prove?* In a word, yes. The first sentence gives a background for the answer by saying that the way in which women tend to look at themselves and at other women is set by their culture's ideal of beauty, and the following sentence gives an example. The next sentence tells about the consequences women face by not living up to this ideal; it's followed by two sentences that talk about the part played by the media in our society in setting an image and conveying the need to measure up to it. Finally, the last sentence in the introduction gives the answer itself: that society, mainly through the media, encourages women to judge themselves according to an artificial ideal of beauty. This answer is the same as the one in the conclusion, and it's clear from it and the rest of this paragraph that the introduction of Jasmine's essay does what an introduction should do.

3. *What points do the paragraphs talk about?* When you read the body paragraphs you can quickly see that all of them develop some aspect of the answer. If you take any particular paragraph in the essay, you can probably relate it to one of the points in either the conclusion or the introduction.

4. *Are the paragraphs arranged in any kind of order?* If you look at how the paragraphs "move" throughout the essay, you can say this: paragraph 2 deals with the media's role in influencing women to measure up to a particular ideal of beauty; paragraph 3 gives a specific example of this type of influence by showing its effect on adolescent girls; paragraph 4 builds on this idea by showing its effects on adult women and the lengths to which

they go to live up to the standard; paragraph 5 extends the range of the problem to include corporations and industries and also puts the focus squarely on women's negative reactions to this influence. Finally, paragraphs 6 and 7 talk about the effect of the drastic lengths many women go to in order to fit the image. Paragraph 8 points out the difference between the statistics of the "ideal" model's body and those of the average woman's body; it concludes by emphasizing that such an image is an unreasonable one for women to strive for and that they shouldn't give in to the media's (and society's) expectations. The "movement" that you notice in these ideas is logical and goes in a cause-and-effect pattern from discussing (1) the idea of the media's influence to (2) examples of that influence to (3) reactions to the influence to (4) the effects of the reactions.

5. *Are the paragraphs connected to each other?* In the section "Moving from One Paragraph to Another" in this chapter, you looked at words that let you relate ideas or move from one idea to another. Does Jasmine use any of these words? Not really. What she does instead, though, is similar; she provides connections between ideas by using the first sentence in a paragraph to connect to an idea in the last sentence of the previous paragraph. Here's an example. The last sentence of paragraph 2 says that, from a very young age, girls are taught that there is a connection between success and their appearance; then the first sentence of the next paragraph says that this connection is particularly apparent to adolescent or teenage girls. By using this type of transition throughout the essay, Jasmine is able to link her paragraphs so that they move her ideas along the line of her thinking.

6. *What can you say about the tone?* After reading this essay, you should be able to identify the style as having formal characteristics. The presence of words like "myth," "culture," "societal," "preoccupation," "media"; the absence of either contractions or colloquialisms; and the number of long, complex sentences show that the style is purposefully formal and right for such essays.

Where, then, does this analysis lead? What can you conclude about this essay? Well, based on the answers to these questions, it should be clear that Jasmine's longer essay really does the same things that you saw in the shorter essays. Her essay is the same as these shorter essays because they all state what they're trying to prove, they introduce their answer, and they provide evidence to back up their answer. The only real differences are as follows: (1) for her essay, Jasmine did quite a bit of research (for which she supplies a bibliography — but more on this in the next section) and (2) she did more thinking and writing than she would have if this had been only a short essay. That's it. Otherwise, longer and shorter essays are exactly the same.

☼ HIGHLIGHTS

- The longer essay, like the shorter one, is still only an answer to a question.

- Like the shorter essay, the longer essay has a conclusion, an introduction, and a number of body paragraphs (the number of these depends on how much you need to write for any assignment).

- The greater number of body paragraphs means that more writing has been done, which, in turn, means that more thinking has been done as well.

- The longer essay is usually an assignment for which you need to do research and for which you need to give documentation of your sources by using a bibliography.

✍ THINGS TO DO

1. Discuss "Body Image" in class. Go through the list of questions in the Spot Check after the essay and deal with them even more thoroughly than you've considered them there. Look specifically for more examples to give for question 3; give more detail about the paragraphs within each of the categories at the end of question 4; and show more cases of connectors or transitions in

question 5. Also talk about your particular ideas about longer essays by asking these questions:

- Have you ever written a longer essay?
- How did you feel about having to do it?
- Was it something you enjoyed doing?
- On what topic and for which course did you write it?
- How did you go about it (in terms of research, reading, thinking)?
- Was it different from writing a shorter essay?
- Which do you prefer? Why?

2. Bring to class a longer essay that you've written or one you're working on now. Compare what you're doing in your essay with what Jasmine did in hers. Think of ways you'd change yours or hers to make it a shorter essay. Then think of what you'd need to do to make either one a longer essay.

3. Read a longer article in a magazine, newspaper, or journal. Then apply the questions in front of Jasmine's essay to that article. Does the article actually answer a question? Try to make it shorter without destroying its meaning. What did you take out? Was it significant information or not? Compare your answers with those of another student who has read the same article.

WHY BOTHER WITH FOOTNOTES?

At some point, you may have asked yourself, "Why should I bother with footnotes? After all, isn't it *my* ideas you want to know about, not someone else's?"

Well, right you are. It is your ideas, your answers, that your teachers want to read about. *You and your thinking are what matter whenever you write an essay.* Every time you work out a response to a topic, come up with ideas to back up that response, and then write it all out, you get a chance to show someone else what and how you think. That's the whole point of writing essays.

As you know, though, it's possible to show someone your thinking on an *informal* or on a *formal* level. For instance, when you're asked to write something on an informal level, chances are that you'll have enough general knowledge about the topic that you'll simply be able to apply some common sense thinking to it and come up with an interesting and reasonable answer. For those kinds of writing assignments, you'll be able to handle them well enough on your own.

But as you saw in "Finding Your Topic" in Chapter 3, there will be other writing situations for which you'll have to do more. Because no one is an expert on every subject, everyone has to do the scouting and digging that are necessary to be able to say something meaningful about them. That's where research comes in.

It's easy to view the books or articles you use as research material as "someone else's work." You might see it as something you have to "go through" to please the teacher and complete the assignment. In other cases, you might see this material in another way: as a source of information to be "borrowed" when you feel you don't have any worthwhile ideas of your own to give.

Instead of looking at research or *secondary source material* (the text that you use for any particular course is your *primary*, or main, source of information) in a negative way, it's more constructive to see it as something positive that can help you give a better answer.

You can take the first step in looking at it this way by remembering what you thought of doing research in "Finding Your Topic" and "Coming Up With Ideas" in Chapter 3. In those sections, you thought about your source material as a *means to an end*. The goal, or "the end," at which you want to arrive is *the best answer you can give*; the way to get there, or "the means," often involves using other people's knowledge and ideas to increase your understanding of a subject. In this view, secondary sources can help your own learning grow.

The temptation, though, is to look at this material as a *substitute* for your own learning. You could think: "Hey, I don't know all this stuff, but here's someone who does. I'll read this over and, just by reading it, it'll become my knowledge, so I won't have to refer to it." The result is that you end up quoting ideas that aren't yours and trying to pass off work that isn't yours; consequently, you could be accused of cheating. This kind of academic cheating is called *plagiarism* (passing off someone else's work as your own), and it can cause you to fail a course or, more seriously, to be expelled from a college or university. The sad part about such an outcome, though, is that it's only the result of a negative way of dealing with other people's material; if you just had a different perception about it, such an outcome wouldn't need to happen at all.

Let's say that you have a positive idea about all the research material that's out there because you see it as a source of information that can help you. You also know that there's a "down side" for not giving credit for your sources either in citations or a bibliography. You begin to suspect that there's a benefit, or an "up side," to giving that credit — and you're right. There are several actually.

★ KEY POINTS

1. One practical benefit is that you avoid doing something you're not supposed to do. If plagiarism carries only negative consequences, then why set yourself up for it? It's that straightforward: if you don't do it, you can't be accused of doing it. In addition, merely by giving references you can actually be rewarded in terms of your mark. Remember, teachers *love* to see sources.

2. By listing your references, you get to show your reader that *you know how to use someone else's ideas.* You show that you have a clear sense of the difference between other people's ideas and your own and that you can use theirs to support yours; this ability, in turn, tells your reader that you are in control of your material and your thinking.

   This is what Jasmine shows in "Body Image"; she separates her ideas and those of the authors she has read and uses their ideas to support her own. Thus, she gives a strong sense to her readers that she's in control of her own thinking as well as that of others.

3. By using someone else's ideas to back up your own, you're bringing in an authority in the field to substantiate your own claim. This is invaluable in getting people to agree with what you have to say. People respect the voice of authority, so find the experts in that field and get them to help you out. Look at this example.

   Say that you bring home a new boyfriend. Your parents look at the leather jacket, tattered jeans, scuffed motorcycle boots, and rainbow-coloured hair style, and they are not impressed. You decide to make an appeal: "But, Mom, Dad — Tiger is really a responsible kinda guy. He got outta high school with an 'A' average, he just got a job sellin' insurance at $20 an hour, and he's already saved $50! And he's doin' all this to show me he loves me cause we wanna get married next month."

   At this point, your parents' reaction to Tiger moves instantly from cool to frigid and stays there. Just then, Tiger's high-school principal strolls in and announces that, yes, indeed, he did get an "A" average in high school and was actually an all-round good student. No sooner are your parents mildly warming to this news than Tiger's manager at the insurance company walks in and declares that Tiger is "a good find" because he's an able and willing insurance seller who'll go far in the business. Then in comes Tiger's bank manager who says she's amazed by Tiger's diligence in fulfilling his financial responsibilities.

Given these assurances, your parents' mood toward Tiger has thawed considerably — but, a wedding next month? At this point, a stranger comes in, congratulates Tiger, and hands him an official notice of inheritance to the part of the family fortune that's been held in trust until today, his 21st birthday. You look around and are somewhat surprised to see your parents heatedly hugging Tiger. There are smiles, handshakes, and "glad ta know ya's" everywhere, and suddenly the wedding plans are being moved from next month to next week!

Even in this humorous example you can see the value of bringing respected views to back up your own.

What you need to do now is look at some practical ways of blending other information or views with your own to get as effective and smooth a result as you can. What you'll do is *incorporate someone else's material* into your own writing as support. Since there are two ways to do this, it's not that complicated.

SPOT CHECK

One way is through *direct quotation*. What this means is that, when you're writing something, *you quote the exact words of an author from a book or article for support*. Say that you're working on an essay about how different writers look at writing. You want to bring in a quotation by Stephen King as an example of one writer's view. Here's how you would do it (the first sentence is yours):

Stephen King, meanwhile, has a somewhat practical view of writing as something that is simply part of a person's range of interests: "Writing is a catch-as-catch-can sort of occupation.

All of us seem to come equipped with filters on the floors of our minds, and all the filters have differing sizes and meshes. What catches in my filter may run right through yours. What catches in yours may pass through mine, no sweat" (King, xii).

What you've got here is about as basic a method for using someone else's material as you'll come across. Your sentence (from "Stephen King" to "range of interests") introduces the idea of what King thinks about writing; then the colon(:) signals to the reader to "watch out" for what's coming next; the quotation marks after the colon say "pay attention ... there's something different here ... it's someone else's words"; the words themselves, if they're less than four lines of your own text in length, should be given exactly as they are; finally, the punctuation and second set of quotes tell the reader "that's it ... we're moving away from the quotation now." The references in the brackets to the author's last name and the page number (in this case it's in Roman numerals) are the preferred "shorthand" way of presenting such information within your own writing (we'll look at fuller details in bibliography references shortly). That, then, is how to handle a direct quote; the only change you'd make to this method would occur if the quoted reference was longer than four lines of your own text. In that case, you'd use what's called *a block quotation*, single spacing and indenting the quoted material while leaving out the quotation marks:

> Stephen King, meanwhile, has a somewhat practical view of writing as something that is simply part of a person's range of interests:
>
> > Writing is a catch-as-catch-can sort of occupation. All of us seem to come equipped with filters on the floors of our minds, and all the filters have differing sizes and meshes. What catches in my filter may run right through yours. What catches in yours may pass through mine, no sweat. All of us seem to have a built-in obligation to sift through the sludge that gets caught in our respective mind-filters, and what we find there usually develops into some sort of sideline.... The sludge caught in the mind's filter, the stuff that refuses to go through, frequently becomes each person's private obsession.

> In civilized society we have an unspoken agreement to call our obsessions "hobbies" (King, xii).
>
> You'd leave a double space and go back to your own writing after the quote. You don't need to use quotation marks for this kind of quote because setting it off like this already says to your reader, "Pay attention to this; it's different from my own words."
>
> The only other thing to notice here is the use of ellipses (the four dots after "sideline") — they tell the reader that something's been left out (usually an example or some less important information you don't need). You'd use three dots to show what's been omitted and a fourth dot as a period if that's the end of the sentence.

Another way to incorporate someone else's material is the way Jasmine did in "Body Image." This method is called *paraphrasing*. The prefix "para" means "beyond," so you could say that to paraphrase means to go "beyond the original words"; in short, what you do is rephrase, or summarize, the author's ideas by putting them into your own words. Doing this lets you make your points and support your idea without reproducing the author's exact words. You would want to use an exact quote, though, when the author says it so well that using the quote would be more effective than putting it into your own words. Again, remember that, like a direct quotation, a paraphrase is also a specific reference to another person's ideas, so you'd follow it with an acknowledgement of the author's last name and the page number in brackets.

When you use these methods of giving credit to your authorities, feel free to use either one or the other at any time, depending on whether you want to make a quiet reference or want to highlight it because it's special.

The last thing to say about secondary sources has to do with footnotes (references that appear at the bottom of any page of your essay) or endnotes (the same ones but listed instead at the end of the essay). These kinds of references are now being replaced by the kind of shorthand notations we saw earlier — (King, xii). This type of abbreviating saves much repetition of information about your sources. You would give a full accounting of the information about your reference sources, though, in the bibliography.

The bibliography, or "Works Cited," section comes at the end of your essay and is a listing of the books, articles, and any other sources you use in your essay. It's important to give this information, because, like the identifying marks of "name, rank, and serial number" in the army, these details aren't just frivolous or unnecessary — what they do is provide your readers with the exact specifics about publication details so that they can identify the source clearly when they need to check on it. In fact, a reader who is well acquainted with the research in a particular field can even look at your bibliographic details and judge whether or not you've included the "top guns" in that area. Therefore, providing this information is important so that people can make qualified assessments of your work.

A bibliographic entry presents the details of your source in a logical and formal order that looks like this:

King, Stephen. Night Shift. New York: Signet Books, 1979.

The information begins with the name of the author — the creator of the book or article; it's formal because it gives the surname before the first name; then it highlights the second most important piece of information, the title; the title reference is also presented formally because it's either underlined or italicized; then, toward the end of the reference, come the concluding details about the book — the place where it was published, the name of the publishing company, and the date it was published. The formality of the entire reference is conveyed by the use of periods throughout to separate the three important areas of information (author, title, and details of publication). It's that simple.

Some of the most common types of bibliographic references follow shortly. These will be handy for most cases, but it would still be a good idea to buy a style guide so that you'll have a full and varied range of style options. These are two of the most useful ones:

Gibaldi, Joseph, and Walter S. Achtert. *MLA Handbook for Writers of Research Papers*. 3rd ed. New York: Modern Language Association, 1988.
Turabian, Kate L. *A Manual for Writers of Term Papers, Theses, and Dissertations*. 5th ed. Chicago: University of Chicago Press, 1987.

Finally, remember that there's no reason why you can't or shouldn't turn your use of secondary sources into a strength for your essay. Rather than look at others' work as an intrusion into your own or as a source of ideas to be passed off as your own, see it this way instead: if your work is already good without theirs, think of how much better it will be with the experts' thoughts supporting your own.

COMMON BIBLIOGRAPHY REFERENCES

1. A book with one author:

   Vonnegut, Jr., Kurt. *Breakfast of Champions*. New York: Dell, 1975.

2. A book with two authors:

   Zborowski, Mark and Elizabeth Herzog. *Life Is with People: The Culture of the Shtetl*. New York: Schocken Books, 1971.

3. A book with two editors (if there were only one editor, only the first person's name would appear):

   Park, Michael and Jack David, eds. *Replay: A Canadian College Reader.* Toronto: Methuen, 1981.

4. A newspaper article with the author's name:

   Duncanson, John. "Student drug use down." *The Toronto Star.* 20 Nov. 1991: A4.

5. A newspaper article without the author's name (the "B2" here and the "A4" in the last reference show the section and page number of the paper in which the article appears):

   "Latest Benetton ad campaign bound to raise unholy ruckus." *The Toronto Star.* 5 July 1991: B2.

6. A newspaper editorial without the author's name:

   "No contest, Canada." Editorial. *The Toronto Star.* 21 Feb. 1992: A20.

7. A magazine article:

   Jennings, Nicholas. "For the record: Hymns and hot tunes." *Maclean's* 18 Nov. 1991: 76.

8. A TV program:

   "The Coneheads' Episode." *Saturday Night Live.* NBC. New York, New York. 22 Feb. 1992.

9. A personal interview:

   Gould, Matt. Personal Interview. 25 Dec. 1989.

☼ HIGHLIGHTS

- It's your thinking that is of prime importance in any essay.

- Sometimes, though, especially in formal writing situations, your thinking can be helped by including secondary sources to back it up.

- The benefits of using references include showing to your reader that you're in control of your thinking and giving the views of expert authorities to support the points you're making.

- Direct quotation and paraphrasing are the ways you'd incorporate your sources into your own material.

- Citations to your sources are given in a shorthand form throughout your essay following your references; bibliographic references are listed on a separate page at the end of the essay.

- Using your sources well can improve your writing and your marks.

THINGS TO DO

1. Have a class discussion about secondary sources, and use the following questions as starters.
   - What's your attitude concerning secondary source material?
   - Is it fair to describe some students' views of it as "a pain" or "unnecessary"?
   - Do students tend to see this material as something to just "help themselves to" and pass off as their own?
   - Why or why not?
   - Does it make sense to look at this material in the way you have here?

2. Discuss some of the courses for which you'd use secondary sources. What are the expectations and views of the teachers of those courses regarding secondary sources? Do you agree with them? Why or why not?

3. If you've already taken the library tour suggested at the end of "Coming Up With Ideas" in Chapter 3, what did you learn from the tour that could be helpful in your discussion of these sources? Perhaps it would be a good idea to have a library worker come to your class to talk about what he or she thinks about students' views of secondary sources.

CHAPTER 5

MAKING YOUR ESSAY WORK

THE TOTAL PICTURE — DOES YOUR WRITING SAY WHAT YOU WANT IT TO SAY?

With every essay you write, there comes a time when you ask the big question: "Is this it? Does this really say what I want it to say?" What you're actually doing here is stepping back and looking at the total picture called *your essay*. You're looking at all the parts — introduction, body, conclusion — and asking yourself if they all "hang together," if they all add up to express your answer completely, if what you've written truly says what you want it to say.

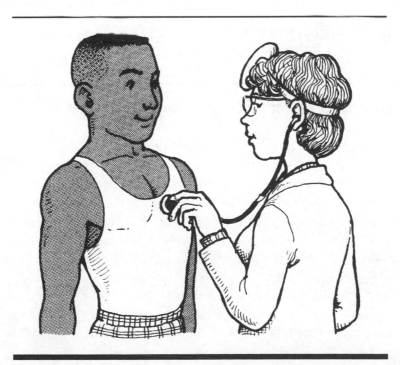

It's like going to your doctor for a checkup. The doctor tests your weight, blood pressure, cholesterol levels, and so on to determine if you're healthy. Checking the "rightness" of each of these "parts," your doctor can then say whether or not the total picture — you, the patient — is a "picture of health."

You, too, can perform this kind of "diagnosis" on your essays. Like the doctor, you have to be able to relate each of the parts you're testing back to the big picture. In other words, *when you know exactly what your answer is*, you can test each part of your essay in terms of that answer.

Let's look at how you can check your essays to make sure that everything adds up. Here's an essay by Ramesh, a student, that deals with the creation of the Superman comic books. Read through it carefully and, as you're reading it, ask yourself these questions:

1. Does the introduction suggest what the answer is?
2. Do the body paragraphs develop the ideas in the introduction?
3. Does the conclusion state strongly what the answer is?
4. Do all the paragraphs "add up"? That is, do the introduction and conclusion give essentially the same answer, and do the body paragraphs support that answer?

If you answer yes to these questions, then the total picture is accurate — the parts all relate to each other, and you can really say that the essay says what you wanted it to say; if no, then the total picture doesn't add up, and the essay doesn't completely say what you wanted it to say. When this happens, you've got to spot the part that doesn't work and change it so that it does say what you mean.

Siegel and Shuster — Superman's Real "Parents"

If I could go back in time and meet anyone from history, I would like to meet the artist team of Joe Shuster and Jerry Siegel. Siegel and Shuster happen to be the creators of Superman, the comic-book hero. I would like to visit Siegel and Shuster because of what they have achieved through creating Superman: they took an idea and created an American "institution" out of it, their idea helped create a strong public interest in science at the time, and their idea became a modern-day legend based on biblical references.

Americans seem to have a talent for taking something created by the "common folk," such as Coca-Cola or McDonald's, and making an "institution" out of it. This is what happened in the creation of

Superman comics. Siegel and Shuster were both art students just before World War II. They were fond of comic books and had often thought of creating the ultimate superhero. One night, in their dormitory, they did just that — they came up with the idea for a superhero and called him Superman. In the beginning, Superman was not a success when it came to getting him printed on the comic-book pages. However, in 1939, King Features Syndicated, a well-known publisher, decided to print the first Superman adventure in *Action Comics*. Since then, Superman has become an American success story. After 50 years, the same publisher still carries *Superman* and the first issue — in "mint" condition, of course — is currently valued at $140,000.

Because Siegel and Shuster had created a character that is scientifically oriented (i.e., he's from the imaginary planet, Krypton), the public's interest in science at that time was given a major boost. Scientific topics such as UFOs, space technology, aviation, aerodynamics, and technological advances in general were all shown to be interesting to people because of Superman. In the comics, Superman is an "alien" who can fly and reach speeds faster than the speed of sound. Such scientific ideas have become even more acceptable in today's society than they were back then. Today, we are beginning to accept the possibility that there are other life forms in space and we have created the Concord, a plane that can fly at speeds faster than the speed of sound.

Although Superman is clearly a modern-day or futuristic hero, the actual story line in the comics seems to have similarities to the life of Jesus Christ in the Bible. Both Siegel and Shuster claimed that any religious similarities are purely speculative or accidental. Yet it is hard to escape the fact that Jor-El, Superman's biological father on Krypton, had sent the infant Superman to earth where his chief mission would be to fight evil while living with his earth "parents," Jonathan and Martha Kent. Similarly, in the Bible, God (Jesus' father) sent Jesus to earth to live with Joseph and Mary, his earth parents, to restructure its evil ways. It is clear that these similarities, whether they are accidental or not, show that Superman is meant to be a modern-day saviour for the earth.

Superman has now celebrated more than 50 years of publishing. He has been constructed and "reconstructed" over this time so that, nowadays, instead of tackling his conflicts effortlessly, he sweats and grunts just like an average human being. However, his ideology remains intact: he still upholds "Truth, Justice and The American Way." By persevering in creating a comic-book hero whose legend is based on biblical tradition yet who elevated the role of science in the modern world, Siegel and Shuster deserve a medal of commendation.

☺ SPOT CHECK

Well, what can you say about this essay on Superman? Does the introduction suggest the answer and provide the reasons or main points for it? Do the body paragraphs say something meaningful about each of those points? Does the conclusion state the answer in strong terms? The answer to all of these questions is, of course, yes. Whether you agree with the points or not, *and whether you like the essay or not,* isn't the issue. What *is* important is this: does the essay "hang together"; are its main points reasonable; and do they make sense? Again, the answer is still *yes,* but let's look more closely just to be sure.

What does Ramesh state as his answer in the introduction? Well, he says that Siegel and Shuster are special to him because of what they created and how they met the challenge in creating it. So far, so good. Then he goes on to give three reasons for why he believes this answer: first, they took a mere idea and turned it into an American tradition; second, their idea fuelled an interest in science; and, third, their idea created a new legend with features similar to those of an old legend.

Now you have to ask, "Are these ideas all related to each other and to the answer?" and "Are they given in any particular order?" It soon becomes clear from looking at the points that point 1 talks about the development of the idea (how Superman comics became as significant and valuable as they are today), point 2 talks about what the idea promoted (that the comic books encouraged people's interest in science), and point 3 talks about the nature of the idea itself (that the legendary basis for the idea is in biblical tradition). Are these points related to each other? Of course they are. They all talk about the same idea (Superman and the creation of the comic book) and, because they do so, you can say that they're "on topic."

It's important to notice here, however, *that although these points are strongly connected to the central idea, they also discuss different aspects of that idea.* That is, they aren't just three points on the development of the idea, or on what the idea promoted, or on the nature of the idea. They could have zeroed in on any one of these aspects, but Ramesh probably had his reasons for wanting to develop different points for his answer.

Now that you've seen how Ramesh's points are related to each other and to the answer, the next thing you should ask is, "Are they presented in the best order?" To check this, you have to ask some questions about the answer and its points. For one, "What is the main focus of the answer"? Is it on Siegel and Shuster or is it on Superman? "A bit of both" could be the answer here, but isn't the focus really on Siegel and Shuster? To Ramesh, they are important because of what they created, and at the beginning of the essay he tells us he wants to meet *them.*

Since Siegel and Shuster are the more important focus, perhaps point 1 (which highlights their achievement), should actually come in the position of the strongest point, point 3. Then, logically, point 3 (which tells about the nature of the idea) should become point 1 because, as a starting point, it makes you familiar with why the idea itself is important. It would then make sense to follow point 1 with point 2, which goes on to show the power of the idea to influence people's thinking.

Let's try out this shift in a moment to see if it makes more sense. Before doing so, though, let's ask if the conclusion states the answer strongly. You don't have to look too far to see that, while most of the sentences in the last paragraph deal with the lasting quality of Superman as a tradition, it's the last sentence that underlines the importance of what Siegel and Shuster accomplished and how Ramesh thinks they should be rewarded.

Let's now look at the reconstructed essay.

Siegel and Shuster — Superman's Real "Parents"

If I could go back in time and meet anyone from history, I would like to meet the artist team of Joe Shuster and Jerry Siegel. Siegel and Shuster happen to be the creators of Superman, the comic-book hero. I would like to visit Siegel and Shuster because of what they have achieved through creating Superman: they took an idea and created a modern-day legend based on biblical similarities, their idea helped promote a strong public interest in science at the time, and they took their idea and created an American "institution" out of it.

Although Superman is clearly a modern-day or futuristic hero, the actual storyline in the comics seems to have similarities to the life of Jesus Christ in the Bible. Both Siegel and Shuster claimed that any religious similarities are purely speculative or accidental. Yet it is hard to escape the fact that Jor-El, Superman's biological father on Krypton, had sent the infant Superman to earth where his chief mission would be to fight evil while living with his earth "parents," Jonathan and Martha Kent. Similarly, in the Bible, God (Jesus' father) sent Jesus to earth to live with Joseph and Mary, his earth parents, to restructure its evil ways. It is clear that these similarities, whether they are accidental or not, show that Superman is meant to be a modern-day saviour for the earth.

Because Siegel and Shuster had created a character that is scientifically oriented (i.e., he's from the imaginary planet, Krypton), the public's interest in science at that time was given a major boost. Scientific topics such as UFOs, space technology, aviation, aerodynamics, and technological advances in general were all shown to be interesting to people because of Superman. In the comics, Superman is an "alien" who can fly and reach speeds faster than the speed of sound. Such scientific ideas have become even more acceptable in today's society than they were back then. Today, we are beginning to accept the possibility that there are other life forms in space, and we have created the Concord, a plane that can fly at speeds faster than the speed of sound.

Americans seem to have a talent for taking something created by the "common folk," such as Coca-Cola or McDonald's, and making an "institution" out of it. This is what happened in the creation of Superman comics. Siegel and Shuster were both art students just before World War II. They were fond of comic books and had often thought of creating the ultimate superhero. One night, in their dormitory, they did just that — they came up with the idea for a superhero and called him Superman. In the beginning, Superman was not a success when it came to getting him printed on the comic-book pages. However, in 1939, King Features Syndicate, a well-known publisher, decided to print the first Superman adventure in *Action Comics*. Since then, Superman has become an American success story. After 50 years, the same publisher still carries *Superman* and the first issue — in "mint" condition, of course — is currently valued at $140,000.

Superman has now celebrated more than 50 years of publishing. He has been constructed and "reconstructed" over this time so that, nowadays, instead of tackling his conflicts effortlessly, he sweats and grunts just like an average human being. However, his ideology remains intact: he still upholds "Truth, Justice, and The American Way." By persevering in creating a comic-book hero whose legend is based on biblical tradition yet who elevated the role of science in the modern world, Siegel and Shuster deserve a medal of commendation.

Well, how does this essay strike you? Is it clearer than the other one? Does it make more sense to move from "the idea" to "the idea's effect" to "the significance of the achievement"?

The main point here is this: once you've written out your answer and its points as your essay, don't assume that it says what you think it says. You've got to do more than that; you've got to go further by "checking it out." A little fine-tuning can go a long way. And how upset would you be if an essay you wrote and put a lot of time and effort into got a "C" when, with a bit of extra analyzing and questioning, it might have earned a "B," or even an "A"?

☼ HIGHLIGHTS

- Check your essay to be sure it actually says what you think it says.
- Check all the "parts" to see if they relate well to each other.
- Check to see if the introduction actually states what your answer is and if the conclusion states the answer strongly.

- Check the body paragraphs to make sure that they develop the main points you've given to back up your answer.

- See whether or not the body paragraphs are in the best possible order, and change them if you think they could be in a better order.

- Don't be afraid to ask questions about what you've written so that you can keep trying to make it as clear as you can.

✍ THINGS TO DO

1. Discuss Ramesh's two essays in class. Talk about the kinds of things you've looked at here. For instance, which of the two essays do you prefer? Why? Does there seem to be a point in changing them or is it a waste of time? Be specific in your comments.

2. In small groups in class, discuss an essay you recently wrote. Does it present "the total picture"? Deal with the questions about the introduction, body, and conclusion that you asked about Ramesh's essays.

3. Do the same as in question 2 with an article in a newspaper or a magazine.

DON'T BE AFRAID TO MAKE CHANGES

Many people tend to think that if something is written down — especially if it's in a newspaper, magazine, or book — then *it must be true*. Well, if this is the case, then think about what's printed in *People* magazine, Harlequin romances, or the *National Enquirer*. Can all of *that* be true?

People are also inclined to see something that's printed as *permanent*. Once the word or the sentence is on the page, they think it's unchangeable. But is this really true?

Both of these ideas — that the printed word is true and that it's unchangeable — say something about how you look at language. For example, when you use language when you speak, you generally don't have such lofty ideas about it. Whatever you may say in one minute, you're free to ignore or contradict the next. You don't feel as tied down to the language you use in speech as you do when you write it.

To test this out, just think of the last time you discussed something in a class; during the discussion people made points, restated their positions, changed their minds, and debated others' viewpoints. The language — and the ideas it represented — was "fluid," moving, changing. Nothing seemed to be "carved in stone."

Now think of how you would use language if you were asked to write about some aspect of that discussion. If those words are to be "nailed down" on the page, you think, they'd better be the "heavy-duty," important-sounding ones, so that they will best express the significance of your thoughts. Once they are on the page, *no one* (even you) should *think* of changing them.

These attitudes about writing are particularly true when it comes to writing essays. When you or the other students in your class write an essay, everyone thinks: "Will mine be good? Will mine be the *right* answer?" "Oh, I've written that already so I can't possibly *change* it."

Well, neither of these ideas "holds water." For one thing, there is no one *right* essay. As long as you've got a reasonable answer, as long as you've got your facts straight, and as long as you write it fairly well, your essay should be as acceptable as anyone else's. Both of you could have different answers, different facts, and different writing styles, but both of you could get an "A."

Why? Simply because it doesn't come down to "right" or "wrong," "true" or "false." It makes more sense to say that an essay can do well if it's a reasonable answer, if it's backed up with points that relate to it, and if it's written well. Then it will be *a good answer*, the best one you're capable of producing.

Instead of asking, "What if my essay isn't the *right* answer?" you should ask, "What if my essay isn't a *good* answer?" To see what the difference is, let's consider how an essay makes a "good answer." Then look at what you can do if you think that the essay you've written isn't a good answer or if you feel that you can come up with one that's a *better* answer.

As an example, let's look at Shakespeare's play, *Macbeth.* You've probably encountered *Macbeth* in high school, since many teachers consider it Shakespeare's most accessible play, the one that's easiest for students to "get into."

Macbeth himself is portrayed in a "larger-than-life" way as a nobleman and warrior, but he is also ambitious and ruthless when it comes to seizing power. His wife, Lady Macbeth, is single-minded in her lust for power, even to the point of pushing Macbeth on when he briefly considers committing murder. Throw in violence, hallucinations, witches, castles, ghosts, and a string of murders each more grisly than the one before, and it's easy to see why *Macbeth* is so popular.

Let's take a brief look at the plot of *Macbeth* before thinking about what to write about it. The story takes place in Scotland about 900 years ago.

Macbeth has just fought in a battle for Duncan, the King of Scotland, and is praised as a courageous fighter. For Macbeth's bravery, Duncan wants to reward him with a new title, Thane of Cawdor. When leaving the battleground (but before finding out about his new honour), Macbeth and his friend Banquo meet three witches who predict the future of both men. They say that Macbeth will become "Thane of Cawdor" and also "King of Scotland" and that, while Banquo himself will never be king, his children and their children will be. Although Macbeth doubts his prophecy, he soon is made Thane of Cawdor; only then does he start to see himself fulfilling the witches' promise to become king.

But since he's not related to Duncan and since Duncan doesn't appear ready to die of natural causes, Macbeth decides to "move things along" by killing Duncan. Duncan just then announces a visit to Macbeth's castle and, by doing so, gives Macbeth the immediate opportunity to carry out the murder. When Macbeth hesitates, Lady Macbeth spurs him on. On his way to stab Duncan in his sleep, Macbeth sees the image of a bloodied dagger hanging in the air in front of him, pushing him on. To avoid suspicion falling on himself, Macbeth kills two of Duncan's servants after he smears their clothes with blood while they're asleep. In the panic following the murder, Macbeth also tries to pin the crime on Duncan's two sons, Malcolm and Donalbain, who themselves run away to avoid (as they suspect) being killed by him.

After this murder, Macbeth starts to become jealous of the witches' promise that Banquo's children will become kings, thereby displacing him, so he hires murderers to cut Banquo's throat. Banquo's son, Fleance, escapes in the ambush. Then, in order to lash out at Macduff, another nobleman who suspects that Macbeth murdered Duncan, Macbeth has Macduff's servants, wife, and children killed while Macduff is away. While Macbeth visits the witches again to find out if he can be beaten in battle, Macduff gathers forces to attack him. Meanwhile, Lady Macbeth goes insane and dies because she can no longer cope with the guilt of all the killings for which she shares responsibility.

Finally, Macduff and his soldiers attack Macbeth's castle. Macbeth and Macduff fight each other with swords — Macduff wins the fight and kills Macbeth. He cuts off Macbeth's head and brings it to Malcolm as proof that Macbeth, the "ambitious murderer," has been killed. This act of vengeance restores order in the kingdom.

That's the story in the proverbial nutshell. Macbeth, a noble and respected man at the beginning of the play, gradually changes in character to become totally devoid of conscience or fear as he kills person after person in his quest for power.

Now that you recall what happened, let's see if you can come up with a reasonable answer to this essay topic: "Is Macbeth responsible for his own actions or not, and how do you view him?"

First of all, you would think about what happens in the play and about how it happens. You might then come up with this response: "I think that Macbeth *is* responsible for his own actions and that, because of this, he shouldn't be pitied." Your reading of certain things in the play led you to this conclusion, so you write out the following essay.

Macbeth — A Willing Killer

Throughout Shakespeare's play *Macbeth*, the central character, Macbeth, commits one murder himself and has several others committed for him. This much is fact. The question that needs to be asked, though, is whether or not Macbeth is responsible for these murders, whether or not he kills willingly. Some people may say that Macbeth's "spirit" to commit murder is an unwilling one, that others lead him to carry out his foul deeds. But certain things in the play point in the other direction: they say that Macbeth himself is responsible for making his own choices and that, because of this, he should not be pitied. The events that show this view the best are the ones that lead up to the three murders — those of Duncan, Banquo, and Macduff's wife and children.

In the case of King Duncan's murder, there can be little doubt that Macbeth's mind is made up to kill his king. When Duncan names Malcolm, his son, The Prince of Cumberland and heir to his estate, Macbeth becomes openly jealous of Malcolm's good fortune: "The Prince of Cumberland! That is a step on which I must fall down, or else o'erleap, for it in my way lies. Stars, hide your fires; let not light see my black and deep desires: The eye wink at the hand; yet let that be which the eye fears, when it is done, to see" (1.4.49–53). Macbeth's desire to kill Duncan is clear here, as it is when he tells Lady Macbeth that his mind is made up: "I am settled, and bend up each corporal agent to this terrible feat. Away, and mock the time with fairest show: False face must hide what the false heart doth know" (1.7.79–82). Later, just as he is about to go into Duncan's room to stab him to death, Macbeth hears a bell ring and states his firmest expression of his intent to kill: "I go, and it is done: the bell invites me. Hear it not Duncan, for it is a knell that summons thee to heaven, or to hell" (2.1.62–64). He then goes into Duncan's room and murders him. What all of these expressions of Macbeth's intention add up to is a picture of a man who knows exactly what he needs to do in order to get what he wants and who does it intentionally and without remorse.

Macbeth is at least as single-minded and cold-blooded when he comes to having his good friend, Banquo, murdered as he is when he kills Duncan. Spurred by suspicion and jealousy, Macbeth plots the deaths of Banquo and his son, Fleance. He tells Banquo about a royal banquet he is planning and says that he wants Banquo there as a special guest; no sooner is this done, though, than he meets with two hired killers and tricks them into setting a trap for Banquo and Fleance. When they agree to commit the murders, Macbeth makes his resolve known: "It is concluded: Banquo, thy soul's flight, if it find heaven, must find it out tonight" (3.1.141–42). When, later, at the banquet, Macbeth is informed by one of the murderers that Banquo's throat has been cut, Macbeth praises the murderer: "Thou art the best o' th' cutthroats. Yet he's good that did the like for Fleance; If thou didst it, thou art the nonpareil" (3.4.18–20). Wanting also to praise the killer who murdered Fleance, Macbeth is told that Fleance has escaped; upset that that has happened, he nevertheless checks to be sure that Banquo is indeed dead and, when he is reassured, replies: "Thanks for that" (3.4.28). While Macbeth is upset to see Banquo's ghost appear at the banquet later, it is clear from the things that he has already said that his intention to have Banquo (and Fleance) murdered is a conscious, intentional choice — and planned this time without any consultation with his wife.

So is it, too, with Macbeth's last and most cold-blooded order to kill — the murders of Macduff's wife and his children. Realizing that he cannot undo what he has done, Macbeth makes the decision to go forward into even more killing to protect his position. He is totally determined to go ahead with his most vicious crime yet in order to injure Macduff by killing those he loves: "The castle of Macduff I will surprise; seize upon Fife; give to th' edge o' th' sword his wife, his babes, and all unfortunate souls that trace him in his line. No boasting like a fool; this deed I'll do before this purpose cool" (4.1.150–54). Macbeth has murderers stab Macduff's wife and children to death; later, Macduff is told that they were "savagely slaughtered" (4.3.205). Macduff's grief shows how enormous a crime this is. His first reaction is almost a step into madness: "He has no children. All my pretty ones? Did you say all? O hell-kite! All? What, all my pretty chickens and their dam at one fell swoop?" (4.3.216–18) His response quickly changes to a mixture of sorrow and anger: "But I must also feel it like a man. I cannot but remember such things were, that were most precious to me. Did heaven look on, and would not take their part? Sinful Macduff, they were all struck for thee! Naught that I am, not for their own demerits but for mine fell slaughter on their souls. Heaven rest them now!" (4.3.221–27) Macbeth's murder of this innocent and defenceless woman and her children is yet another deliberate step he takes in covering up his original crime, Duncan's murder. But this murder, like Duncan's and Banquo's, is a decision made consciously by Macbeth and another for which he is entirely responsible.

What Macbeth's speeches and the events leading up to these murders reveal, then, is a single-minded sense of purpose behind his actions. He sets his sights on becoming king illegally and never swerves from his goal — and he continues to kill to preserve his gains. As a result, it is impossible to feel any sympathy or pity for such a man. At the end of the play, Macbeth's noble stature is seen again as he takes a chance fighting Macduff and being killed instead of serving Malcolm, the rightful heir. But even here we are reminded of Macbeth's calculating misdeeds when Macduff condemns him: "I have no words: my voice is in my sword, thou bloodier villain than terms can give thee out" (5.8.6–7). Shakespeare's focus on Macbeth is never lost: all the good that Macbeth might have done because of the nobility of his nature, he says, has been totally blotted out by all the evil actions for which Macbeth is responsible.

Works Cited

Shakespeare, William. Macbeth. Ed. Sylvan Barnet. New York: New American Library, 1987.

SPOT CHECK

When you finish writing this essay, you might stop to think: "Hey. Not bad. This really says what I wanted it to say." Then you check it over and find that it indeed "hangs together": the conclusion and the introduction state the answer (in different ways), and the paragraphs develop and support the reasons for your answer.

But do these things make this essay a "right" answer or a "good" answer? Is it the only answer you could have given? Or is there a better one?

Well, let's think about these things for a moment. First, let's ask if you'd want to change or improve this essay at all — to come up with a different or a better answer. You've read the play and you've become familiar with Macbeth's character. Your first response to the essay question was that Macbeth *is* responsible for his actions and is, therefore, not to be pitied. Then you sat down and wrote this essay. But as you worked on the essay and as the essay question turned over in your mind, you started to look at the issue in a different way. Perhaps a case could be made for the other side; perhaps Macbeth is *not* responsible for his actions and is therefore to be pitied. Maybe it was what the witches said to him and maybe it was Lady Macbeth who led him on and influenced him to do "the dirty work."

You might now be thinking, "These kinds of thoughts only present a problem." After all, you've got an essay that holds together and expresses a reasonable point of view. "Why not just leave it alone in spite of my new ideas?" Besides, you think, "I don't have the time to change it even if I wanted to."

But let's say you do have time, and that you're intrigued by your new ideas — maybe they're closer to the answer you'd like to give than the ideas in your first essay are. So what do you do?

Well, if you have the opportunity, it's probably a good idea to make the change, to improve your whole answer. Now you have to look at the words on the page and see that *you can change them if you want to.* Remember, the words only reflect your thinking — if your thinking changes and you come up with a better idea, then it's necessary and acceptable to change your words. They're not "carved in stone."

Here's the new essay that you go on to write about Macbeth. Look closely: maybe you can use some of the words from your original essay.

Macbeth — An Unwilling Killer

Throughout Shakespeare's play *Macbeth*, the central character, Macbeth, commits one murder himself and has several others committed for him. This much is fact. The question that needs to be asked, though, is whether or not Macbeth is responsible for these murders, whether or not he kills willingly. Some people may say that Macbeth's "spirit" to commit murder is a willing one, that he carries out his foul deeds single-mindedly and in cold blood. But certain things in the play point in the other direction: they say that, as an unwilling victim of the influence of others and of his own mind, Macbeth is not responsible for making his own choices and that, because of this, he should be pitied. The events that show this view the best are the ones that lead up to the three murders — those of Duncan, Banquo, and Macduff's wife and children.

In the case of Duncan's murder, there can be little doubt that others play a large part in influencing Macbeth's actions. In the first of the important events that lead Macbeth to kill Duncan, Macbeth had been told by the witches that, in addition to being Thane of Glamis, he will also become Thane of Cawdor and King of Scotland. Although Macbeth does eventually kill Duncan to become king, Banquo makes clear just how much the betraying influence of the witches is a factor in Macbeth's action: "And often-times, to win us to our harm, the instruments of darkness tell us truths, win us with honest trifles, to betray's in deepest consequence" (1.3.123–26). Yet while the power of the witches' suggestions is important, it would probably lessen in Macbeth's mind — except for the fact that it is strongly reinforced by his own wife, Lady Macbeth. She is determined to go through with the deed by holding Macbeth to his word: "I have given suck, and know how tender 'tis to love the babe that milks me: I would, while it was smiling in my face, have plucked my nipple from his boneless gums, and dashed the brains out, had I so sworn as you have done to this" (1.7.54–57). Macbeth finally cannot stand up to this pressure, so he agrees to kill Duncan. Even on his way to do so, though, the pressure to kill does not give up. Instead, it takes on a new form — a hallucination of a bloody dagger appears in Macbeth's mind, urging him on: "is this a dagger which I see before me, the handle toward my hand? ... art thou but a dagger of the mind, a false creation, proceeding from the heat-oppressed brain? ... Thou marshal'st me the way that I was going" (2.1.33–42). What all of these expressions of influences on Macbeth add up to is a picture of a man who is strongly pressured by other forces — both external and internal — that push him to do what they want him to do: giving in to them, he becomes an unwilling victim in committing murder.

This pattern holds true in Banquo's murder as well. Here, though, Macbeth is primarily led by the suspicion and fear in his own mind. Macbeth's fears of Banquo show up frequently: "There is none but he whose being I do fear" (3.1.54–55). When Macbeth is told that Banquo has been killed in the ambush that Macbeth had set up, he is relieved; however, he becomes extremely agitated in the next moment when he learns that Banquo's son, Fleance, has escaped: "Then comes my fit again: I had else been perfect ... but now I am cabined, cribbed, confined, bound in to saucy doubts and fears" (3.4.22–26). These "doubts and fears" that haunt Macbeth have caused him to act irrationally in killing Banquo, and, at the royal banquet, they cause him to externalize his inner fear in front of all his guests when he sees Banquo's ghost: "Thou canst not say I did it. Never shake thy gory locks at me" (3.4.51–52). Macbeth's guilt overwhelms him here as he tries desperately to banish the guilt that the ghost represents from his sight: "Avaunt! and quit my sight.... Take any shape but that, and my firm nerves shall never tremble.... Hence, horrible shadow!" (3.4.94–106) While it is true that Macbeth has Banquo killed, it is also true that he does so because he has no control over the fear, suspicion, doubt, and guilt in his overworked mind.

In a similar way, Macbeth is the victim of the internal workings of his own mind and the external prophecies of the witches when he comes to ordering the deaths of Macduff's wife and his children. After Banquo's death, Macbeth acknowledges that his mind is full of strange ideas that seem to control him: "Strange things I have in head that will to hand, which must be acted ere they may be scanned" (3.4.140–41). Desperate, Macbeth talks with the witches, the "weird sisters." His paranoid fears are so intense by now that he wants to make absolutely sure that no one can take his power away or kill him. When he asks the witches to tell him who can harm him, they answer, Macduff, "The Thane of Fife" (4.1.72). In order to strike out at Macduff in his absence, Macbeth orders the deaths of his "second choice," Macduff's wife and children: "The castle of Macduff I will surprise; seize upon Fife; give to th' edge o' th' sword his wife, his babes, and all unfortunate souls that trace him in his line" (4.1.150–53). Macduff's family is unfortunately killed as a "consolation prize" because Macduff had fled the country. This is less a case of Macbeth deliberately setting out to kill them, than it is one of following the suggestions of his mind and the witches; Macbeth even realizes that, in a strange kind of way, he has become the witches' "pawn." He then condemns them and those who pay attention to what they say — himself included: "Infected be the air whereon they ride, and damned all those that trust them!" (4.1.138–39) Finally, near the end of the play, Macbeth makes it clear just how far he has been led past what can be considered "normal," past the "point of no return": "I have supped full with horrors. Direness, familiar to my slaughterous thoughts, cannot once start me" (5.5.13–14). The murders of Macduff's wife and children are caused by those "slaughterous thoughts," which themselves are caused by the internal forces in Macbeth's mind and the external forces of the witches. Macbeth is just the victim of their influences.

What Macbeth's speeches and the events leading up to the three murders reveal, then, is the extent to which Macbeth is really an unwilling murderer. He struggles against the forces in his own mind and those in the world at large that combine to put unbearable pressure on him. As a result, he becomes a victim of these forces and someone who is to be pitied because of their control of him. Even at the end of the play, Macbeth shows how deep the influence of the witches still is in his mind; Macduff has just told Macbeth that the witches' predictions of safety for Macbeth are untrue and the effect on Macbeth is so great that he loses his courage: "Accursed be the tongue that tells me so, for it hath cowed my better part of man!" (5.8.17–18) Shakespeare's focus on Macbeth is never lost: all the good that Macbeth might have done because of the nobility of his nature, he says, has been sadly lost because Macbeth chose instead to listen to the voices of the witches, his wife, and his own mind's fears.

Works Cited

Shakespeare, William. Macbeth. Ed. Sylvan Barnet. New York: New American Library, 1987.

🛑 SPOT CHECK

All right, you've changed your essay and improved your answer. You first saw as the chief issue in the play that Macbeth *was* responsible for his own actions (in which case he could be accused of a major crime such as first-degree murder); you then rethought your answer and decided that, when all the evidence was in, he really *wasn't* as cold-blooded as he seemed at first. So you took what you thought was a *better* position and argued that it's more reasonable to see Macbeth as a victim of other forces (in which case he could only be accused of the lesser crime of second-degree murder). Bear in mind, too, that these may not be the only choices for presenting this issue; you may have started with your second choice and ended up re-thinking it and going to your first (or to any other reasonable case). Whatever the options, though, these essays on Macbeth are similar to what you saw in "The Court Case." To balance Lisa Leegull's defence of Kristy Kleer, you could imagine a prosecuting attorney arguing the other side of the issue. In Macbeth's case, you argued *both* sides. You chose to present one of them because you thought it was closer to the way things really were.

Remember that your choice between the two essays is not arbitrary or frivolous. What you've got here are two genuine cases that can be made for the same essay topic. You choose one over the other because you think that it better expresses the situation. Great. Then go ahead and make the change. But if you ask which one is the "right" one, the answer is, "they both could be."

Unlike the trial in "The Court Case," where there can be only one de-cision — either guilty or not guilty — here the situation is different. Both essays on Macbeth could do well as long as they give a good answer. Remember that it isn't a question of "right" or "wrong" as much as it is one of "good" or "bad." What you're doing in any essay is trying to give *a good answer*: one that's reasonable (that makes sense), that's backed up with points that relate to the answer, and that's well written. That's all anyone can ask for any essay. Both *Macbeth* essays are good ones if they do those things well.

A final reminder about changing an essay is this: "If it feels good, do it." What's important about making changes, though, is to do it if it provides you with a better answer. In fact, you *should* do it if you can. Always give the better or the best answer you can. Your brain isn't frozen; it's thinking of ideas all the time. The ideas for the later essay were bubbling in your mind at the same time you were thinking of the earlier one, so you don't have to wonder too much about where the new answer and the new points came from.

The last word here concerns the language. When your ideas change, then the language that you use to express those ideas won't be far behind. You might ask, "Will I find the words to say what I think?" This shouldn't be a problem; as often as not, the words will find you. And don't be reluctant to use some of what you wrote in your first essay: recycle as much of what you wrote, as long as it makes sense. If it doesn't, don't use it.

☼ HIGHLIGHTS

- Be more concerned about finding a *good* answer in your essay than coming up with the *right* answer.

- A good answer is one that is reasonable, has supporting points that relate to each other and to the answer, and is well written.

- As long as time allows, change your answer if you come up with a better one.

- When you change your answer you'll have to change your language too; just remember to "economize" by recycling whatever you reasonably can.

📣 THINGS TO DO

1. Reread the essays on Macbeth and discuss them in class. Consider these questions:

   a) Are the introduction, body, and conclusion of each essay related?

   b) If they are, does this make the essays good answers?

   c) As far as you can tell, are these essays reasonable answers?

   d) Which one makes more sense? Which do you agree with more?

   e) How are they different from each other?

f) Which words, sentences, parts of sentences, or quotations have been recycled?

g) Is it reasonable to have recycled them? Do they make sense in their new context?

h) In general, how do you feel about the changed essay? How would you feel about doing this to your own essays?

2. Take an essay that you've written either in class or for an assignment and rewrite it using a different answer (even if you don't agree with it). Then discuss it using the same questions you used in question 1.

3. Rewrite an article in a newspaper or magazine giving a different answer. Discuss it using the same questions as in question 1.

CHECK YOUR SENTENCES — ARE YOU SAYING IT THE BEST WAY YOU CAN?

In the last two sections you looked at making changes to your paragraphs and even your whole essays. You looked at "the big picture" and parts of the big picture to make sure you were saying exactly *what* you wanted to say. Now let's look at *how* you're going to say it. Let's look at "the little picture" — the sentences themselves — to make sure that you're using sentences effectively and that your ideas are as clear as possible.

By looking at your sentences and thinking about how you can best write them, you're doing something similar to what you did in the section "How Are You Going to Say It? — Choosing Your Tone" in Chapter 3. There, you thought about the language you use to express yourself in different situations. And here you're doing something like that as well. Instead of focusing on the words, though, you're "zeroing in" on your sentences; you're looking closely at how you're writing them, so that they'll help you make your thoughts clear.

What you should think about first, then, is this: "What kind of sentences are you talking about? And for which kind of essay?" As you saw in the section on tone, you're likely to write only two kinds of essays — formal or informal — both of which have different characteristics. In spite of the differences, however, in both types of essays you'd use *complete* sentences — *sentences that contain a complete thought.* You might use incomplete, chopped, or fragmented sentences in some cases to show "street talk," but you'd use quotations marks to indicate that they're different from the complete sentences that you're using throughout the essay.

But what is a "complete thought"? Aren't all of your thoughts "complete"? And how can you tell the difference between a "complete" and an "incomplete" thought?

A complete thought or sentence that expresses a thought is one that is "whole," *one that is made up of all its important parts*. You can also say that, in thinking or writing, *a sentence must have all of its important parts so that it makes sense*. Otherwise, you're left with only part of an idea that likely won't make sense at all.

But what are these sentence parts? How many of them are there? And how can you check if they're there or not?

This is where you have to look at "what a sentence is." You also have to look at what a sentence *is not* — by looking at the three situations in which sentences may look complete but really aren't:

1. subject and verb agreement errors
2. fragments
3. run-on sentences.

If you can learn to spot these three types of problem sentences before handing in your essays, then you will stand a good chance of boosting your marks.

Before we look at these faulty types of sentences, though, let's think about what makes a sentence complete. If you know this, then you'll be able to check for "completeness" in any and all of your sentences. While there are many parts to any sentence, there are only two parts that have to be in every sentence you write: *a subject and a verb*. You've probably heard this before, but it's so important that it's worth repeating. And the reason it's so important is this: if you can find the subject and the verb, you'll have the key that will let you fix any of the "big three" sentence errors.

So what is a subject and what is a verb? Every sentence is about someone or something and that's the *subject*. It's almost always a noun (a person, place, or thing) and it tells you "who" or "what" this sentence is about. A *verb* is related to the subject because it describes the subject or shows the action that the subject does — a verb is the word or words that tell what the subject *does* or what it *is*.

🐾 SPOT CHECK

Look at this sentence: Water drips. What is the verb? If you're looking for an action or description, then you've got something that shows action (something happening) in the word "drips." Now, if the subject tells "who" or "what" does the dripping, then the only choice can be "water" (not a bad choice, since it's the only other word in the sentence). So "water" is the subject and "drips" is the verb. It's that straightforward. But it's not always that simple. More often than not, in order to give complete, fleshed-out ideas, the sentences you write are longer and more detailed than just two words. But, if you start to see how things work with short, simple sentences, then you'll also be able to figure things out in longer ones. Try these sentences:

Day changed to night.

The moon is high.

Dogs bark.

The end was near.

In the sentence, "Day changed to night," you can see that the action word (that is, what happens or what the subject does) is "changed." Now you'll ask "who" or "what" changed and see that the only word that makes sense when it's connected with the verb is "Day." So the subject and verb together (which make up the sentence in its simplest sense) are the logical combination of "Day changed" (the rest of the sentence — "to night" — just says what became of the day, what it changed into).

The same applies to the next sentence, "The moon is high." Here, the word "is" (a form of the verb "to be" — am, are, is, was, were) tells that something in the sentence is being described (that is, it says something about the nature of the subject — "He is ill"; "She was happy"). Then you ask "who is?" or "what is?" and the only reasonable answer is "moon" — the moon is what is "high."

It's the same for the next two sentences. "Bark" or "barking" is clearly an action, so it must be the verb. Again, you have to ask "who bark?" or "what bark?" The only answer is "Dogs," so it must be the subject. And, in the last sentence, "The end was near," "was" describes the subject. The only answer that makes sense when you ask, "who was?" or "what was?" has to be "the end."

Finding the subject and verb in a sentence is important if you are to know whether a sentence is correct or not. All you need to do is ask some basic questions about any sentence. And the most basic and meaningful of these questions are "what is?" or "what is being done?" and "who or what relates to the verb?"

The true link between any subject and any verb is based on common sense, on being able to see the logical connection between them. That's all there is to it.

As you know, the major difficulties in writing sentences lie with three types of sentence errors: subject and verb errors, fragments, and run-ons. If you can spot and improve these important sentence mistakes when you make them, you will write a better essay and be able to raise your essay mark considerably. Correcting these errors is straightforward enough as long as you can identify the subjects and verbs. Let's see how this works.

SUBJECT AND VERB AGREEMENT

In the short sentences you've looked at, you've already checked them for agreement. *Agreement* means that, when the subject and verb are put together, they *make sense,* or *agree.* Perhaps the most important common sense idea about subject and verb agreement is this: *a singular (one) subject needs to go with a singular verb; a plural (more than one) subject needs to go with a plural verb.* If you're not sure which is which at any time, it's a good idea to say them out loud and listen closely. Many times you may not know the exact rule, but you can still know by hearing if the subject and verb sound right together. Let's go back to the previous examples.

When you put the subject "moon" together with the verb "is," they make sense or agree; if you were to put the word "moon" with another verb such as "am," "are," or "were," that combination wouldn't make sense because those two words don't agree: "moon am" or "moon were" are combinations that just aren't right when they're put together. The same applies to the next sentence, "Dogs bark." The subject and verb make sense when they're together because the subject "dogs" refers to more than one dog (plural) and is connected to the verb "bark," which is the verb form used for plural subjects. To test this, try combining the plural subject "dogs" with the singular form of the verb and you'd get "dogs barks" — clearly something that doesn't sound right or make sense.

All right, so far, so good. But, unfortunately, not all subject and verb agreement errors are this obvious or easy to spot. When you consider longer sentences, for instance, you may find that they contain "word situations" that aren't as easy to identify as the examples you just looked at. By doing the same kind of common sense thinking as you have been, though, you should be able to make sense of them, too.

MULTIPLE SUBJECTS AND VERBS

"More than one subject" or "more than one verb" are two such situations. Many of the sentences you write will have only one subject and only one verb, but not always. Sometimes you'll write a sentence with several subjects and one verb, sometimes with one subject and more than one verb, and sometimes with more than one subject and more than one verb. Here's a sentence with *one subject* and *more than one verb*:

> The sailors smoked and drank all night in the musty bar.

Looking at the verbs first, you can quickly spot two action words, "smoked" and "drank." When you ask "who" smoked and drank, you see that it's only the one subject, "sailors" — "sailors smoked and drank." So the *single* subject does *two* things.

Now let's look at a sentence that has *more than one subject* but *only one verb*:

> Madonna and Michael are pals.

Here you see that "are" describes a condition and you ask "who are?" The only logical answer is that both "Madonna and Michael are" ("pals" just tells you what they are). In this example, you see *two* subjects being described by *one* verb.

In the third situation, you can have *several subjects* and *several verbs*:

> Wrestlers Mad Dog Vachon and The Masked Marvel leaped from the ropes and jumped on poor Randy Savage.

The action words are easy enough to identify here — "leaped" and "jumped" — and the only logical response to answer "who leaped?" and "who jumped?" are the subjects "Mad Dog Vachon" and "The Masked Marvel." In this example, you've got *two* subjects doing *two* things.

Most of the time, checking your sentences for agreement when you're using multiple subjects and multiple verbs is easy enough to do. There are other subject and verb agreement situations that you'll have to watch out for, though.

MULTIPLE NOUNS REFERRING TO ONE PERSON

One of these occurs when you use two nouns to describe one person.

> His helper and lover is the same woman — his darling wife.

Here, the words "helper" and "lover" look as though they're two subjects in search of the plural verb "are." But, since both words refer to *one* woman, you'd use the single verb "is" to relate to them.

INTERRUPTIVE PHRASES

Some phrases provide a similar illusion. When a phrase like "as well as," "including," "along with," or "in addition to" appears connected to the subject, you might be tempted to combine it as a plural subject needing a plural verb. You won't, though. These formations look like they're part of a multiple subject, but they really don't form part of it (remember that only the conjunction "and" can be used to form a multiple subject).

> *Sesame Street*, as well as *The Muppet Show*, is still a popular TV program.
>
> Drink, along with drugs, is a dangerous thing.
>
> All my children, including the youngest, are simply perfect.
>
> Love, in addition to adultery, is a common theme on many afternoon soaps.

In each of these sentences, the phrase only "interrupts" the flow of the main sentence itself, so it can't logically be seen as part of the subject — no matter how much you may want to see it that way.

PREPOSITIONAL PHRASES

Another source of confusion is when a group of words called a *prepositional phrase* comes between the subject and the verb. Such a phrase can contain a noun that comes right before the verb, and your natural tendency would be to take that noun as the true subject when it isn't. Remember that a preposition is a word that usually tells about the location or direction of something: about, above, before, beneath, beyond, down, except, from, in, near, of, off, on, out, past, since, through, under, within, are some examples of prepositions.

> His idea of dining out is a salami and a six-pack.
>
> The patients under anesthetic were sawn open.

Both of these sentences have a prepositional phrase: "of dining out" in the first one and "under anesthetic" in the second. You might want to say that "dining out" is the subject of the verb "is," but the subject is really "idea": "His idea is a salami and a six-pack" (admittedly, the sentence sounds better with the phrase "of dining out" in it because the phrase gives fuller meaning to the sentence). Although prepositional phrases contain words that sound like they could be the subject, don't look for the subject in prepositional phrases: they never contain one.

The same goes for the other sentence. Without the prepositional phrase "under anesthetic," you're left with "The patients were sawn open." The subject of the verb "were sawn" can only be "patients," not "anesthetic." The same is true when the noun in a prepositional phrase is plural:

> One of the dangerous dudes spit chewing tobacco right on Slim's new, white, velvet-covered cowboy boots.

The prepositional phrase "of the dangerous dudes" contains a noun ("dudes") that comes immediately before the verb "spit," so you might reasonably think that the sentence reads "the dangerous dudes spit." But the phrase "the dangerous dudes" really just describes the real subject, "one." So the sentence simplified reads, "One spit chewing

tobacco." The subject is actually the singular subject "one," not the plural noun "dudes."

SUBJECTS JOINED BY "OR" OR "NOR"

Subjects connected by "or" or "nor" should be joined with singular, not plural verbs. This only makes sense. If you say "apple or orange," you mean one *or* the other, not one *and* the other. Since the subjects are thought of separately, then the verb should logically agree with the subject closest to it. The same holds true for a combination of "either ... or" and "neither ... nor."

> In the book, *Dracula*, a juicy spider or savoury flies provide a
> tasty snack for the insane character, Renfield.

In this case, "or" separates (not combines) the singular subject "spider" and the plural subject "flies." Because "flies" is closer to the verb "provide," the verb is in its plural form. If the subjects were reversed, then it would be "spider provides." But you wouldn't join the subjects in a plural combination because you're using "or" instead of "and."

"EVERYONE," "ANYONE," "SOMEBODY," "ANYTHING"

Although they may look like they're plural, words such as "everyone," "anyone," "somebody," "anything" (and any other forms of these) are really singular. The clue here is in the fact that the endings of these words — "one," "body," and "thing" — are singular.

> Everybody loves somebody sometime.

The test here is in the verb "loves" — it's in the singular form (she loves, he loves) so then "everybody" must be singular in order to agree with it.

COLLECTIVE NOUNS

Collective nouns may strike you in one of two ways: when all the members of the group act together, it's as though they function as one subject, and so they need only a singular verb. However, when they act as individuals within the group, they function as several subjects, and they need a plural verb.

> The crowd is moving toward the movie stars as they move toward the limousines.
>
> The crowd are heading home happily with their fantasies fulfilled.

In the first sentence, the individuals in the subject, "crowd," act together as a singular subject for the singular verb "is moving"; in the second sentence, individuals in the subject, "crowd," act separately as a plural subject for the plural verb "are heading" (each is going off to his or her own home).

SENTENCES THAT START WITH "THERE" OR "HERE"

Sometimes you'll write sentences that begin with the word "there" or "here" and follow it naturally with a form of the verb "to be": "There is," "Here are," "There were," and so on. When you do this, don't take "there" or "here" as the subject. Instead, use the verb that follows these words to find the subject by asking "who is?" or "who are?"

> There are many ways to smell a rat.
>
> Here is one of them.

In the first sentence, the word "There" is not the subject, but it's directly followed by the verb "are." Now ask yourself "who are?" or "what are?" and the only reasonable answer can be the noun "ways." So the subject is "ways" and the verb is "are"; you can test this out by rethinking the sentence in its awkward-sounding, but natural, order: "Many ways are there to smell a rat." The same is true of the second sentence. "Here" is not the subject, but it's followed by the actual verb "is." When you ask "who is?" or "what is?" your only answer can be "one": "one is." Again, test this out by changing the order: "One of them is here."

INVERTED SENTENCE ORDER

In the previous case, you looked at changing the order of a sentence. As sometimes happens, you'll write a sentence that is "turned around" or "inverted" and where the subject comes *after* the verb (it most often comes before the verb). But the connection between the subject and the verb still exists.

> In the undergrowth of the ravine, riddled with bullets, lay the gangster's body.

In this example, both the subject and verb come at the end of the sentence, but the verb "lay" comes before the subject "body." Yet the tie between the two is still there; when you ask "who lay?" or "what lay?" the only answer that makes sense is "body."

SINGULAR NOUNS THAT LOOK PLURAL

Some nouns can look as though they're plural because they end in "s," but they're really singular. "Robotics," "news," "mathematics," and "ethics" are a few examples of such words. When you're in doubt about whether these words are singular or plural, look them up in your dictionary.

> Robotics is big business in Japan.

Even though it ends in "s" and therefore looks plural, the subject "robotics" agrees with the singular verb "is."

✍ THINGS TO DO

Work on the following sentences in class. Identify the problem area and then find the subjects and verbs. Compare your answers with those of the other people in class and explain why you made your choices.

1. With the bass pounding out the beat, the band raised the excitement level of the crowd, pitched all into a frenzy, and pleased even its most doubting detractors.

2. One of the reasons are your money.

3. Sammy and Suzie, surely serious students, are also somewhat serious sweethearts.

4. Everybody knows that the lack of love or money presents people with a serious health risk.

5. The dog's owner and provider is Percy, the garage mechanic.

6. Here is the place where the buck stops; there is the place where it speeds up.

7. Aerodynamics are an area of major research for car makers.

8. Neither the warring nor the actual divorce are good for children whose parents constantly fight with each other.

9. Patience, as well as compassion, is a commendable characteristic to possess.

10. The audience is stretching their legs during intermission.

11. Bob, Carol, Ted, and Alice laughed and loved their way through life.

12. Behind their many turbulent years together, under all the rows, bickering, and tears, was an undying affection for each other.

SENTENCE FRAGMENTS

The second of the "big three" sentence problems is the sentence fragment. The word "fragment" means a "piece of" or a "part of" something; in this case, when you apply it to sentences, it means that you've written only *a part of a sentence*, not a complete one. What you usually write in such cases is a group of words that doesn't make up a whole sentence — an *independent* clause — that can stand on its own. What you'll find when you tackle these, though, is that your knowledge of subject and verb agreement can help you considerably when you're looking for and fixing sentence fragments. Remember, while you can and do use fragments quite freely in your daily speech (and see them often in fictional writing), you should use whole sentences that express whole thoughts when you're writing essays.

You usually write a sentence fragment as a group of words that *looks like* a sentence and *is punctuated like* a sentence but which is actually lacking some things: in one case, it could be missing a subject or the whole verb; in another case, it might have the subject and verb, but it still doesn't make up a complete sentence or independent clause. Let's look more closely at these situations.

SENTENCES THAT LACK A SUBJECT OR COMPLETE VERB

When a sentence lacks a subject or the complete verb, the result is a sentence fragment. There are three different instances where this kind of omission occurs.

The first occurs when the subject and verb are *both* missing.

Especially red ones.

What can you say about this? Is there a verb that shows action or description? Is there a subject that "red ones" refers to? You know that "red ones" refers to something, but you don't know what. So, while there's *some* information contained in this group of words, it lacks both a subject and a verb.

The second instance happens when only the *subject* is missing.

> Won't go alone.

Here you can find the verb "go" easily enough. But can you tell "who" or "what" won't go? It's clear that this fragment is missing a subject.

In the third situation, it's the *helper verb* that's missing.

> I going to pub night.

Since the helper verb for "going" isn't here, this doesn't make much sense. What's needed is another part of the verb such as "am" or "was" to logically connect with "going" (I am going, I was going) for this to be right.

DEPENDENT CLAUSES

A fragment can also be created when a sentence has a subject and verb but still isn't complete and can't stand by itself. In this case, it's called a *dependent* clause because, as the word "dependent" tells you, it has to depend on other words in the sentence in order to make sense.

> Because I have to party.
> Although you are very desirable.

You can see that each of these fragments has its own subject and verb — "I have" and "you are" — but it still can't stand alone because of the words "Because" and "Although." These words and others like them (after, before, if, provided that, since, unless, when, whether, which) tell you that you're dealing with a "dependent clause" type of sentence fragment. How can you fix these? An easy way is to simply remove them from the fragments; you'd be left with "I have to party" and "You are very desirable." Depending on what you want to do with the sentence, though, this simple solution may not be preferable. You might want to create a fuller sentence by adding an independent clause — a complete sentence (which doesn't have to be a long one) — to the dependent clause.

> Because I have to party, I can't study.
> Although you are very desirable, I have a headache tonight.

The short sentences "I can't study" and "I have a headache tonight" are complete and, when you add them to the dependent sentences, you form new complete sentences that are not fragments.

✍ **THINGS TO DO**

Correct these fragments and comment on what kind of fragment each is. Then discuss them in class and explain why you chose to improve yours the way you did.

1. Often at The Bay.

2. Because people with brothers or sisters are less likely to develop high blood pressure as adults.

3. I looking for you on the dance floor, but you had left.

4. When TV ads aimed at children exploit youths.

5. Can't wake up early in the mornings.

RUN-ON SENTENCES

As the name suggests, "run-on" sentences are those that run on or run together. In other words, the sentences are complete — the opposite of fragments — but blend together to form something that looks like one sentence but is really made up of more than one sentence. To fix these sentences you have to be able to spot the complete sentences within the run-on and then separate them. Again, being able to identify which subjects agree with which verbs will help you a great deal here.

There are really only two types of run-ons that you need to be able to find and fix: (a) the run-on itself and (b) the comma splice.

THE TRUE RUN-ON

In the true run-on, you find two (or more) sentences that are written together as though they're one:

> Our wedding day was sublime everything was perfect.

You can quickly see that there are two complete sentences here: "Our wedding day was sublime" and "Everything was perfect." The problem, though, is that the two complete sentences are written together as one, with no acknowledgment of the fact that each should stand on its own. You'll look at how to fix this in a moment.

THE COMMA SPLICE

In the comma splice you have two complete sentences that are mistakenly joined by a comma rather than written as two distinct sentences:

> Our wedding day was sublime, everything was perfect.

The relationship between the two sentences is falsely expressed by the comma. The comma joins the two independent sentences together, when in fact they should be apart.

There are a few ways to improve run-on or comma splice sentences without changing them drastically. One way is to make them two distinct sentences by separating them with a period:

> Our wedding day was sublime. Everything was perfect.

Another way also uses punctuation. If the sentences are closely related to each other in meaning, and if you're trying to draw the reader's attention to something important about the relationship between them, you can join them with a semicolon:

> Our wedding day was sublime; everything was perfect.

You can also fix them by joining the two sentences in one complete sentence. In this case, you'd show an equal relationship between the two sentences by co-ordinating, or balancing, them with a conjunction like "and," "but," "or," "nor," "for," "so," "yet":

> Our wedding day was sublime for everything was perfect.

Finally, you can show the relationship between the sentences so that one sentence is dominant and the other is subordinate (one is independent, the other is dependent). To do this, you'd use a subordinating conjunction such as "because," "if," "since," "till," "when," "where," "while":

> Our wedding day was sublime because everything was perfect.

✍ THINGS TO DO

Correct these run-ons and comment on what kind each is. Then discuss them in class and say something about why you chose to improve yours the way you did.

1. Drug dealers under the age of 18 often carry beepers to stay in touch a new law is trying to make this illegal.

2. Elizabeth Taylor is frequently in the news for one reason or another, she's a very popular woman.

3. It's fun to own a pet many say that it's also good preparation for becoming a parent.

4. Holding back anger is not good for people, they do so because they feel a need to be nice.

5. Billy Crystal is one of the funniest actors around so is his buddy, Danny DeVito.

Well, that's about it for the "big three" types of sentence problems: subject and verb agreement errors, fragments, and run-ons. The best "tool" you can use to find and fix any of these is *your knowledge of subjects and verbs*. If you can go through your essay and "weed out" these problems before you hand it in, you should be able to clear up the way you're saying things and boost your mark at the same time.

✍ THINGS TO DO

These sentences are a mixture of the "big three" errors. Identify each error, correct it, and tell why you made that particular choice. Look closely, because some sentences are correct.

1. A Japanese company says it has perfected the ideal toilet to allow Kitty to relieve himself without getting his coat wet an infra-red system starts the flush when the cat leaves and dries the seat for the next time.

2. A U.S. telephone company are now working on a system for patching recorded ads into the four-second pauses between rings in a telephone call.

3. Because depression can lead to sickness.

4. Couples are most likely to argue on Wednesdays, a study found that disagreements are often sparked midweek because it's furthest from the weekend in both directions.

5. The aim of computer companies are to come up with the machine that can carry 1 trillion instructions per second.

6. Saturday morning cartoons been regular viewing for children for decades now.

7. She is a child who won't eat her vegetables.

8. Getting married on a Ferris wheel could be just right after all marriage goes round and round and has its share of ups and downs.

9. As the daylight hours get shorter and the daytime highs get lower.

10. Behind the trees, under the shrubs, the princely frog.

11. It's possible to become a water addict some do by drinking about 80 eight-ounce glasses a day.

12. Most cellular telephone users reports that the portable phones improve everything from their business earnings to their love lives because they can stay in touch.

13. Some psychologists say that the prospect of freezing, bombing, or falling flat in front of an audience are the biggest fear adults feel.

14. There is a bar in Edmonton where the beer is cheap until the first person makes the inevitable trip to the washroom, at that point the price returns to normal.

15. In weekend seminars and workshops, beating conga drums to release their rage, sweating in communal saunas, letting out the wild man inside, the "new" men of the '90s are tapping into their feelings.

16. Neither rap nor rock are satisfactory when what you really need is blues.

17. Since the risk of dying from heart disease is about twice as high for people with fluctuating weight than for those whose weight stays reasonably steady.

18. The Crash Test Dummies made it big with "Superman's Song," they're from Winnipeg.

19. The estate, bordered by water on three sides, has three private beaches and overlooks the harbour.

20. Andrew Dice Clay, the latest in a long line of foul-mouthed, humourless, stand-up comedians.

21. Fifteen toilet plungers, a jacket with a parrot on the shoulder, five non-matching pairs of shoes, and a spider costume with ten legs was stuffed into one medium-sized suitcase.

22. The number of deaths will climb steadily over the next few decades the funeral industry is one which will continue to grow in the coming years.

23. Smuggling cigarettes in a kayak on the Niagara River.

24. A new breed of video pirates are taping films right off the movie theatre screen.

25. The defence argued that the tape of 2 Live Crew was vulgar and offensive but not obscene, the Crown argued the lyrics fitted the legal definition of obscenity because they were dehumanizing and degrading to women.

26. We're living in a time when you can manage your own change a lot of it is attitude but you should look at change as a positive.

27. Because Taster's Choice ads use a soap opera format to sell coffee.

28. Regular bowling, as well as lawn bowling, are excellent pastimes.

29. Don't knock bats conservation groups are now heralding the furry, flying animals.

30. Although some people think that "bald is beautiful."

WHERE TO GET HELP — TEACHER, PEER TUTOR, OR WRITING WORKSHOP?

Essay writing is often viewed as a solitary task. And it's not difficult to see why.

The essay itself is almost always an individual effort. You come up with the essay topic; you grapple with the ideas involved and formulate an answer to the topic; you do the research; and, finally, you write everything out in a clear and neat way for a reader to understand. To most people, essay writing is simply something that a person does alone, without help from anyone else.

For the most part, this idea is true. But this doesn't mean that you can't get help, or that you shouldn't turn to other people for advice. When you write essays alone, it's easy to see yourself as a kind of "student Robinson Crusoe" or as a pioneer on some intellectual frontier — just you and your ideas and that's all. But essay writing isn't really a trip into "the void" or a *Star Trek* journey that goes "boldly where no one has gone before." On the contrary, many others have "gone before." Many people have written essays before and are capable of giving you the kind of help you need.

★ KEY POINTS

1. *One person who can offer you help is your teacher, instructor, or professor.* This may seem like an obvious suggestion to some students and an odd one to others. But really it's neither. Teachers are there, of course, to teach essay writing in the classroom, and that's where you'll pick up most of what you'll learn about essays. But, as you found in "Coming Up With Ideas" in Chapter 3, they're also the first and most obvious sources for help when you need to talk to someone about your particular essay.

   Teachers generally tell you their office hours and when they are available for consultation. And that's exactly what you should *do* when you're stuck or having trouble focusing on your ideas: *Make an appointment and get some advice.*

   Perhaps you think that your ideas are not "sophisticated" enough to tell your teacher about; perhaps you feel you're "just being a bother" to the teacher; or perhaps you're simply shy. Whatever the reason, it's fairly clear that too few students go to their teachers for help with their essays. By not doing so, though, you're failing to take advantage of the most important (because they know you and your work the best) and most immediate (because you see them frequently) person available for help.

   What will your teachers do to help you with your essays? Well, they won't write them for you, but they will help you with any and every aspect that you might be struggling with. For instance, they can get you to sort through some of your ideas to help you work out an answer; they can help you focus and arrange the main points in your answer; or they can help you work out specifics such as tone and sentence structure. It doesn't matter which area might be bogging you down. By asking questions and making constructive comments, your teachers can give you whatever kind of help you need when you need it.

2. Another person who can help you with your essays is a peer tutor. "What," you might ask, "is a peer tutor?" Well, we all probably know what a tutor is, but we may not know that a peer tutor is someone who is your peer, or your equal. In this case, these people are other students who are paid by a college or university to tutor students who need help with their essay writing. Usually peer tutors are "senior" students in their second or third year who already have the experience with essays that new students might not yet have. Peer or student tutors have taken a number of courses for which they've written several essays and, because of this experience, they are already familiar with what's involved in writing an essay and with what their instructors' expectations are. Because of this experience, they're in a good position to give you the "bird's-eye" view of essay writing from the student's point of view. While teachers are an excellent source of help for essay writing, it's the view of the capable student writer that often comes closest to the actual experience of those students who need help with essay writing.

Look at it this way. As you know, you get much of what you learn about essay writing from your teachers — and that's only natural since they're the ones who know the most about what they're trying to help you with. Sometimes, however, there might be some difficulty in bridging the gap between someone knowledgeable and experienced in essay writing and someone who is new to it. This gap could exist for several reasons: (a) it might be the distance between the more experienced teacher and the less experienced student in terms of each one's understanding of an essay; (b) it could be the gulf between the "leader" role of the teacher and the "follower" role of the student; (c) or it could simply be a generation gap. Whatever the reason, these "barriers" can prevent students from learning as much as they can from their teachers.

If this happens to you, it would be a good idea to get help from a peer tutor. As one student helping another student, a peer tutor may be easier for you to relate to and will have writing experience that you can draw on. Another advantage is that, as "senior" students, peer tutors have gained insights into teachers' ideas about essays and so can give new student writers an "insider's" view of what to look for.

Do yourself a favour. If you can't or won't get help with your essays from your teacher, look for a peer tutor. Find out about the peer tutor program at your college or university. You might even look ahead to the future: when you feel capable about and confident with your own essay writing abilities, *you may want to work as a peer tutor yourself.*

3. *A third place to get help with essays is at a writing workshop.* Many colleges and universities have a writing workshop service to help students improve their writing. Writing workshops are staffed by senior or graduate students who — like peer tutors — have had many years of experience writing essays. These workshops are often highly structured, centrally located, and easily accessible. This service is free to students and is usually well advertised on campus.

    When you need help with an essay, go to the writing workshop and fill out a form. You will then be assigned to a specific tutor and book an appointment to see that person. At your first meeting, you will probably discuss your concerns about essay writing in general and the essay you're working on in particular. Once your tutor has an idea about your general needs (be they perception, organization, sentence structure, or grammar) and your immediate concerns (what is the due date for your essay? how much have you already done? what kind of research do you need to do?), the two of you can then work out a plan to tackle both areas.

    For example, if you make an appointment for an hour per week to work with your tutor and if your essay is due in three weeks, you've got a total of three hours to consult with someone specifically about that essay. You and your tutor may decide to use all the time in each hour on a discussion of that particular essay;

or, if some of your difficulties in the general area affect that specific assignment, you might decide to spend 15 or 30 minutes on a discussion of that area and the remainder of the time on specific aspects of the assignment. Later, once you've finished your essay and handed it in, you might reorganize your appointments differently since you don't have the immediate pressure of an assignment.

The idea behind using the writing workshop is to improve your writing gradually. It can be most helpful if you say to yourself, "If I can just do a bit better on each essay by consulting with someone on an ongoing basis, I'll eventually get it." If you've already "got the idea" and are, for the most part, writing good essays, then you might want to use the writing workshop occasionally as a refresher or for "fine-tuning" some aspect of your writing. For the best results, though, even for good writers, the writing workshop shouldn't be a short-term "quick fix."

The writing workshop makes sense for all students. If you're struggling with essay writing and getting poor marks, then the writing workshop is a good place to go on a regular basis to improve your work. Even if you're writing well, though, remember that you can always use the writing workshop to help you change those "B's" into "A's."

☼ HIGHLIGHTS

- Essay writing is often seen as a solitary process.
- Your teacher is the most logical choice for advice about your writing difficulties.
- Another good person to go to for help is a peer tutor, someone who has proven writing ability and who can give you a student's view of how to improve.
- You can also get help from a writing workshop — a place that's full of seasoned writers who will work with you on your essay on a regular basis.

✍ **THINGS TO DO**

1. If essay writing poses problems for you, talk with your teacher about your concerns. What are some specific suggestions she or he can make about improving your writing? Positive reinforcement is an important way to improve. It's fair to ask your teacher to give you helpful comments on your essays (although most probably do) if you're not getting any.

2. Find out about the peer tutor program at your college or university. You can usually do so through an information centre or student union. If you need an appointment, make one. If not, go there when you have some time to spend and take along an essay of yours as a sample of your work. Find out how to sign up. And, if you're serious about improving your writing, try to go regularly.

3. Find out if your college or university has a writing workshop. Drop in and find out what's involved in joining. Make an appointment to see a tutor. Be sure to bring one of your essays. Again, attend regularly and you'll likely see an improvement in your work.

HOW TO HANDLE DEADLINES

Facing deadlines is something that no one really likes to think about or talk about. Monthly bills, the next rent payment, and class assignments are all things with a "due date" attached to them, a date we know is "out there somewhere," but a date that most of us don't really want to face.

Sure, you'd like to do something about deadlines. You'd like to be able to snap your fingers or wrinkle your nose like Samantha in *Bewitched* and get instant results: "There. That's it. It's done." But you know it's not that simple.

Realistically, you know that the job won't get done — that the essay won't be written — until you actually do it. So why don't you? What's stopping you?

Well, some people aren't stopped at all. They take their essay assignments, do the necessary research, formulate a response, balance their time carefully, and hand in a well-presented essay on or even before the actual due date. But who are these people? Are they different from you? Or do they just see things differently than you might?

There's no magical formula to handing in a good essay on time. The only things necessary are a clear idea of what it is you're doing, a good idea of how long it'll take you to do each part of it, and the good sense to get help when you need it. Knowing what you're doing in these three areas can result in an *enthusiasm* for your task and a sense of *pride* in having done the best job possible.

If you don't have these factors going for you, then you could easily become a victim of the kind of fear and desperation that I talked about at the beginning of the book. You're probably familiar — either through your own experience or that of another student — with the kind of scenario that the student who procrastinates or who feels a kind of mental paralysis goes through.

Imagine yourself as this student. You get your essay assignment at a time when many other things are crowding your mind: thinking about how different college or university is from high school, lining up for registration or at the bookstore, wondering what new and exciting people you'll be sitting next to in class. When you hear the due date, it sounds far off in the future: "Wow! Four months away," you think to yourself, "I've got loads of time."

Rather than go right to the library, you decide to do only some preliminary reading in your course textbook and some general thinking about the essay topic. Two months rush by and you notice that some of your classmates have already done some work on their essays. You start

to get a bit concerned. You finally make "the big trip" to the library. But once you start digging into the material on the topic, you discover that the best books are already out — probably taken by your own classmates. So to satisfy yourself that you're actually doing something, you take out some of the remaining second — or third — best choices and bring them home. You flip through some of the relevant sections to see what you might use.

All this time you're "working" on an answer to your essay question (if not on paper, at least in your mind) and are convinced that all you really need is a few days (or even hours) of uninterrupted time to "nail it down." The trouble is that you've also got work due in several other courses, and it looks like the necessary chunk of "uninterrupted time" is not coming your way.

The frustration mounts in the last week, so you make the necessary time and grind out a rough draft of THE ESSAY. The night before the essay is due, you look at the pages that represent the "blood, sweat, and tears" of your endeavours and think mercifully: "Hallelujah! It's done! Something's done. Now I just have to get it into shape."

At the same moment, though, you feel a pang of regret as you realize two things: (1) "Hey! This wasn't so bad at all. In fact, I actually kind of enjoyed it. I wonder how much more I could have enjoyed it if I'd really given it the time and thought I should have"; and (2) "Knowing that this paper is only a 'shadow' of what I could have written — no, of what I *should* have written — I know already that I'll never get as good a mark for it as I would have gotten for the better essay I never wrote."

While this scenario is a bit horrifying, as well as enlightening, it needn't be a situation that you find yourself in. To avoid it, you have to understand how you can help yourself deal with deadlines.

★ KEY POINTS

1. *Have a clear idea of what you're doing.* Approaching your assignments with a clear idea of what you're doing and of how to go about it can help you overcome the fear and uncertainty you might feel toward essay writing. That's what this book has tried to do. It's tried to make the idea of what an essay is as clear as possible, and it's tried to show you how to approach writing an essay in as straightforward a way as possible. Once you understand the idea and once you've practised it a few times, you'll begin to look at deadlines in a new way: as an *opportunity* to show that you can "do your stuff," that you can write a good essay on time.

2. *Know how long you'll need to do each part of the essay.* When you know which parts of the writing process are involved, you'll have to make decisions about how much time you'll need to give to each. For example, if you've been assigned a topic, you've already "saved" the time you needed to think of one. That means you can give that time to other things. If you think back to the imaginary student's scenario of four months, then it would make sense to use half of that time to research, think, and come up with your answer. Then use your third month to write as good a draft as you can. At the beginning of the fourth month, check over your essay to make sure that it really says what you want it to say and make any changes you need to. You might even have the time to let it sit for a few days so that you can get it out of your mind for a while and then come back to it with "fresh" eyes. This kind of break often lets you see things that you might have missed when you were staring at it constantly.

   Although you won't always have four months for every essay you write, it's safe to say that these general divisions apply no matter how long you have to work on one: 1/2 of the total time for research and thinking, 1/4 of the time for writing, and 1/4 of the time for revising, editing, and typing. Apply these time divisions, and you should be able to finish any essay on time and get the best mark you can.

3. *Get help when you need it.* This point can be summed up quite simply: "Don't go it alone if you don't have to." You've already looked at the benefits of getting help with your essays in the last section, but it's worth repeating in our discussion of deadlines. Submitting your work to someone on a regular basis is an excellent reinforcement; if you feel that you're "slipping" in your efforts to keep to your schedule, it's good to have someone in the background gently nudging you on.

In an ideal world, handling deadlines wouldn't be a problem. You would just look at what has to be done and at how much time you have in which to do it. Then you'd figure out how much time you'd need to spend on it each day and, like the Nike slogan says, you'd "just do it." But things don't always work out so neatly. While you may have all the good intentions in the world to do the job on time, events come up or the time just drifts by. It could be a family problem, an unexpected visitor, or a party — or you might just be having a good time with your feet up and the music on. Whatever the reason, you must deal with it, or else you will never have the time you need to do your work. So to help yourself set aside a little time each day in order to stay ahead of deadlines, it's important to look at the time you need for essay writing in a certain way.

One way to look at this time is as "practice time" or "hobby time." You would set aside a certain amount of time each day to practise on a piano (or any other instrument) or to devote to your favourite hobby. So should you also say, "This hour, or half hour, is the time I'm going to spend on my essay each day." It doesn't even need to be that long — even 15 minutes a day is something. Whatever the length of time, it's the "practice habit" that's important. What you're doing is developing a kind of routine that will help you "practise" on your essay a bit each day.

Little by little, over a period of time, you'll be able to see your essay grow. You'll also see that, as you work on it steadily, you'll have a sense of control over your essay and your ideas instead of feeling controlled *by* the essay and the deadline. And don't worry that what you sometimes write isn't "top-shelf" material. If you write something — anything — each day, you'll at least be making progress by staying on target and getting your ideas down. You can always go over it another time to see what you'll keep and what you won't. Just try to set aside a certain time *each* day and stick to it *every* day.

Another way to look at your essay writing time is to see it as a special opportunity to talk to your teacher. When you're in class, you usually share your teacher's time and attention with many other students. If your class is in a large lecture hall, you may never even meet, let alone get to know, your teacher. So when you sit down to work on your essay, it's a good idea to see the essay itself as your opportunity for a kind of "chat" with your teacher to let him or her know what you're thinking about your topic. Instead of seeing your essay as a heavy-duty, serious, intellectual unloading of facts, it's much more helpful to look at it as your personal chance to say something interesting and intelligent to your teacher on a topic you've both read about and talked about.

There are two pleasing benefits to learning to deal with deadlines. The first of these is that you begin to develop a sense of *enthusiasm* for writing. Whether you draw, figure skate, or whistle, the more you do it and the better you get at it, the more you look forward to doing it again. And, while it may sound strange, the more you feel comfortable with essay writing and the more you feel in control of it, the more you'll find yourself actually enjoying the challenge of tackling your next one.

Along with the enthusiasm comes the second benefit — *pride* in your work. The reward of doing a job well is the recognition of others. When you're able to improve your mark from a "D" to a "C" or from a "C" to a "B," your teachers usually recognize your improvement in their evaluation and in their comments. You, in turn, will feel a growing sense of achievement in the fact that you've been able to write your essays and the ideas behind them as clearly and as well as you can.

☼ **HIGHLIGHTS**

- Have a clear idea of what you're doing when you write an essay.

- Know how long you'll need to do each part of the essay.

- Get help from your teacher, peer tutor, or writing workshop tutor when you need it.

- Look at the time you need each day to work on your essay as "hobby time" or "practice time."

- View your essay as an opportunity to have a "chat" with your teacher about the essay topic.

- Don't be surprised if you find yourself becoming enthusiastic about writing essays once you've had some success at it; as well, be prepared to feel a deserved sense of pride in any improvement — large or small — that you're able to make in your work.

✍ **THINGS TO DO**

1. Discuss the scenario of the "imaginary student" in class. How true do you think it might be? Are there any aspects that specifically apply to you? Or are you someone who works well with deadlines? If so, what are some helpful suggestions you could make? What, specifically, has worked for you before?

2. Now that you've finished this book, discuss your ideas about what you do when you write an essay. Are these ideas different from those you had before you read the book? If so, how?

3. Talk about time allocation for research and writing. Are you able to give enough time to each part of the process, or do you feel rushed?

4. Have you gotten help with your essays before? Where? How exactly were you helped? Did you feel your writing had improved? Why?

5. Do you feel enthusiasm for or pride in your essay writing? Why or why not? If not, what do you think it might take for you to feel that way?

DOING BETTER WITH EACH NEW TRY

Many people look at essay writing as a skill. I prefer to look at it as *a way of seeing*. True, there are decisions to be made that require skill — "Is that sentence too long? Are those words just right?" — but even these questions have as much to do with how you see something as they have with judgement and taste. Writing an essay has everything to do with how you understand and respond to things.

If one thing has changed as a result of how you now look at an essay, it should be the way you feel about writing one. If you're more comfortable now with the idea of writing essays, then you've taken a big step from where you were at the start of the book. That's a real accomplishment and something you should feel good about.

Another consequence of your new way of looking at essays may well be the marks you receive. If you've been getting only "D's" for your work so far, it could be that your new knowledge of writing essays will allow you to set your goal at "C" for the next one. Similarly, if you've been getting "C's" on a regular basis, it would be great if you could set your goal up a notch and attain a "B."

But there's no magical formula for instant improvement. This book may help, but change takes time. Learning to see things in a different way and feeling good about it doesn't happen overnight.

You're the one who makes the difference here. You're the only one who can decide whether or not you will actually write better essays. If that's important to you, then you'll keep an open mind to how you can help yourself.

Although you may get discouraged, think about how much more discouraged you would get if you didn't improve your essay writing quickly or even at all. This is where you'll need to understand the idea of *gradual improvement*. This is where you have to think: "My teacher didn't get there overnight, so how can I be expected to?"

Each new try presents you with a new opportunity. Whether you "blew" your last essay badly or only "flubbed" it a bit, the next one gives you

another chance to do better. The next one says: "All right, stay calm. Let's look at what you can improve in your last essay as well as what you did right in your last essay. Let's keep the stuff you did right, and work on what you didn't do well. The result should be an improvement."

At the same time, don't lose sight of what you're doing this for. Improving your marks is a good thing, but it's only a consequence of what you're really doing. What you're really doing when you write an essay is *saying something well.*

The one who benefits from learning to say something well is *you.* Improving your marks is a good thing, but the real reward is being able to say something to your reader simply, clearly, and confidently. The marks you leave behind when you finish school and enter the working world — the rest you take with you into that world.

READER REPLY CARD

We are interested in your reaction to *Common Sense: A Short Guide to Essay Writing* by Bernie Gaidosch. You can help us to improve this book in future editions by completing this questionnaire.

1. What was your reason for using this book?

   ☐ university course   ☐ college course   ☐ continuing education course
   ☐ professional   ☐ personal   ☐ other_____
      development   interest   _____

2. If you are a student, please identify your school and the course in which you used this book.

3. Which chapters or parts of this book did you use? Which did you omit?

4. What did you like best about this book? What did you like least?

5. Please identify any topics you think should be added to future editions.

6. Please add any comments or suggestions.

7. May we contact you for further information?

   Name: _____

   Address:_____

   _____

   Phone: _____

(fold here and tape shut)

MAIL ≫ POSTE
Canada Post Corporation / Société canadienne des postes

Postage paid
If mailed in Canada

Port payé
si posté au Canada

Business Reply

Réponse d'affaires

0116870399   01

0116870399-M8Z4X6-BR01

Heather McWhinney
Publisher, College Division
HARCOURT BRACE & COMPANY, CANADA
55 HORNER AVENUE
TORONTO, ONTARIO
M8Z 9Z9